How to
Your Marketi ﾉﾞ

The Guide to Becoming a
Successful Marketing Student

First Edition

Gary Davies

GARY DAVIES
SALTASH CORNWALL UK

This book is dedicated to Linda, Chris, Andy, mum and dad.

Gary Davies

52 Andrews Way, Hatt, Saltash PL12 6PE

First edition 2011

ISBN-13: 978-0-9567934-0-9

For information on all Gary Davies publications visit the website at
www.garydavies.com/books

Cover designed by Chris Davies

Printed and bound in Great Britain by Latimer Trend, Plymouth PL6 7PY

Contents

Book review and acknowledgements

'This excellent book would be of major use to students studying for a range of marketing examinations and assessments. It is easy to read and has excellent suggestions.

It should help them make a sensible choice about what to study, where and how. The section on instructional words will help students understand exactly what they are being asked to do and remove one of the major reasons why students fail assessments – not understanding the question!

Reading this book should be an essential element of course selection and examination preparation.'

Professor Keith Fletcher MA PhD FRSA FCIM
Director of Education
The Chartered Institute of Marketing

This book would not have been published without the enduring and faithful support of a small but select band of exceptional people.

My special thanks go to my wife Linda and my sons Chris and Andy who have always backed and encouraged me, especially during the most challenging stages of this particular writing project. My eldest son Chris displayed a degree of patience that is simply beyond my understanding, plus he always gave me sound and frank technical advice when needed. I wish I could be as cool and calm as him.

I would also like to record my sincere appreciation for the extremely useful and practical advice provided by Professor Keith Fletcher and for the guidance, technical support and considerable tolerance shown to me by Bob Brown and Keith Jones at Latimer Trend.

Preface

This unique book is the product of more than 20 years research and almost 40 years of successful practical experience in the field.

How to Pass Your Marketing Exams: The Guide to Becoming a Successful Marketing Student was written especially for students of marketing. Readers are provided with clear and valuable guidance on how to plan and manage their own study programme. Students are also introduced to a range of tried, tested and effective examination and assignment preparation techniques.

This book was developed specifically for students who are currently studying, or planning to study marketing at intermediate level. That means if your aim is to gain a formal marketing qualification, such as a professional marketing certificate, professional marketing diploma or any similar certified or professional marketing qualification, this book has been written for you.

The material has also been designed to meet the needs of students who may be required to study a single marketing module that forms an optional or mandatory component of a non-marketing specialised professional qualification, such as a purchasing, banking, media or hospitality and tourism diploma.

This guide can be used effectively in conjunction with any form of delivery programme, including traditional face-to-face classes and intensive residential workshops, or any type of open, flexible, distance or online learning system.

Students enrolled and supported at accredited study centres and also independent marketing students who plan to undertake their studies on a totally self-directed learning basis are equally likely to find the guidance and advice in this book invaluable.

Anyone who is studying for a marketing-related qualification such as e-marketing, marketing in hospitality and tourism, marketing communications, advertising or public relations is also likely to appreciate the numerous study, assignment preparation and examination tips.

In addition to highlighting the indispensable study skills and examination techniques that will enable students to achieve success in their marketing exams, this publication also incorporates a range of marketing exam style questions. These sample questions are specifically designed to provide readers with the opportunity to test their marketing knowledge and practice their question analysis, answer planning and writing skills.

If they wish, readers may submit their completed answers for professional marking and feedback. The marking is undertaken by an experienced and qualified marketing examiner and the answers are returned to the student, together with some appropriate and constructive feedback.

To remind students of the important marketing issues and to assist readers with their research, the key marketing models and topics are listed in the appendices at the end of the book.

About the author

Gary Davies is a writer, trainer, coach and consultant. He has also worked as a chief examiner, senior examiner, examiner and exam marker with various internationally recognised professional institutions.

Gary has also worked in B2C and B2B sales, marketing management and general management. He has lectured in marketing, management and business, managed numerous marketing education programmes and led teams of tutors and examiners.

Based in Cornwall in the South West of England, Gary now places the emphasis on writing and publishing. However, he still remains in contact with students and course delegates by designing and delivering the occasional marketing, sales, management and leadership training programme. He operates worldwide and has worked with numerous students from the United Kingdom, Africa, the Middle East and the Far East.

Gary's considerable practical experience is underpinned by a range of relevant marketing and management qualifications, including the Chartered Institute of Marketing Diploma (DipM) and a Masters Degree in Business Administration.

Notably, following the decision he made some years ago to resign from his secure marketing management job and embark on his own full-time studies, Gary became a successful, award winning mature student.

Chapter 1 – How to use this book

This book is written in an informal, personal style. My main aim is to provide you the reader with clear, worthwhile and easy to follow advice. I also want to encourage you to develop and apply the key study skills, as well as the proven examination and assignment preparation techniques.

Although this guide may be written in a less formal style than some marketing textbooks you might read, don't let the personal approach mislead you. The thoroughly tried and tested professional guidance that follows really can have a positive effect on your examination and coursework results.

While no book can guarantee exam success, I am confident that the advice provided in this book can work for you. I know this because when I was a mature student, I applied all the key principles myself and as a direct result I achieved considerable examination success. Later, when I became a marketing tutor and senior examiner, I passed on the benefit of my own experiences and successes to my students. The subsequent exam results and the positive student feedback received over many years, confirm the effectiveness of the techniques and methods that now form the basis of this book.

Target readership

As mentioned already, the contents of this book were developed specifically for students who are currently studying, or planning to study marketing at intermediate level. The intermediate study level includes professional marketing certificates and diplomas and also single marketing modules.

Anyone who is working towards many of the marketing-related qualifications, such as e-marketing, marketing in hospitality and tourism, marketing communications, advertising or public relations certificates or diplomas, is also likely to benefit considerably from following the advice contained in this guide.

As illustrated in Figure 1.1 students will find the contents of this book indispensable, whether they are undertaking their studies on an open, flexible, distance or online learning basis, undertaking self-directed studies at home, attending intensive residential workshops or face-to-face classes at college or university.

Marketing Certificates (via a professional marketing institute such as the Chartered Institute of Marketing & other institutes worldwide)	**Marketing Diplomas** (via a professional marketing institute such as the Chartered Institute of Marketing & other institutes worldwide)
Marketing Modules (via non-marketing institutes as a part of another professional qualification e.g. CIPS, CIB, IFS	**National Certificates, Diplomas or Degrees** (via colleges or universities involving study at further or higher education level)

Figure 1.1 The marketing qualifications covered by this guide

By the way, the material in this book should also assist marketing undergraduates who need to sit traditional exams, or submit coursework assignments as part of their university assessment programme.

Although some content (such as the material in the sample questions section) is specific to the intermediate level of study, much of the advice and most of the techniques are likely to be relevant and beneficial to all students of marketing.

An outline of the contents of this guide

Before exploring the various study skills and techniques in detail, here is a brief outline of the contents of each chapter of the book.

Some readers may want to start at the beginning and then work through the book from cover to cover. Others may prefer to prioritise specific chapters, or read them in a different order.

Basically, think of this guide as a useful resource that can be consulted when required, depending on your own individual needs and preferences. Of course, the amount of time you have available before the exam will also affect how you approach your reading.

Chapter 1 – How to use this book

Throughout the remainder of this chapter I will suggest how I think you should proceed with your reading, depending on your individual needs and the timing of your exams. I will also outline the main elements and features of this guide, including the submission facility that allows you to answer questions and submit your answers for professional marking and feedback.

Chapter 2 – Courses and study methods

This chapter is aimed at readers who have not yet made the decision to sign up for a specific marketing course or qualification. It incorporates advice on the selection of marketing as course of study and as a career. Chapter 2 also highlights the need to establish the value and credibility of any qualification you plan to gain, as well as the suitability of the proposed study method and the competence of the provider. It also emphasises the need to establish early on precisely how and when your knowledge and understanding of the subject will be assessed.

Chapter 3 – Study planning

In this chapter you will find some advice on developing a study plan, conducting a personal SWOT analysis and participating in a student self-help group, or an informal 'study buddy' arrangement. Chapter 3 also highlights the need to thoroughly check out the syllabus and then schedule and manage your time effectively, so that you can pay the necessary attention to your studies.

Chapter 4 – Effective studying

This chapter outlines the key tasks that new students should undertake in order to give themselves the very best start possible. Advice is provided on note taking, course handouts, undertaking the necessary reading, completing any required coursework and avoiding complacency. Because marketing tends to surround and involve us all (at least to some degree) recommendations are made on identifying and capturing current examples that can be used later to good effect in the exam, or in any suitable assignments.

Chapter 5 – Exam preparation

In this chapter the emphasis is given to exam preparation. Readers are reminded of the need to re-visit the course syllabus document and reading list, to ensure they have not missed out anything important. Suggestions are provided on how you might acquire and analyse the past exam papers and re-assess your strengths and weaknesses. The need to practice your question analysis and answering techniques is highlighted, as is the importance of examination planning so that nothing is left to chance.

Chapter 6 – In the exam

This chapter makes the point that from the very start you should aim to make a positive impression in the exam. It also stresses the need to read the exam paper carefully, manage your time effectively, analyse and address each question, then plan and develop your answer. Advice is also provided on adopting the correct answer format and differentiating your answer from the competition.

Chapter 7 – Answer planning

This chapter explains the reasons why students should carefully analyse questions and prepare an answer plan in the exam, before writing out their answer in full. It also illustrates how to analyse a question and develop an answer plan by utilising a suitable framework. The analysis and planning techniques are applied to a sample question, to fully demonstrate the recommended approach.

Chapter 8 – Case studies and assignments

As case studies are often featured in marketing exams, guidance is provided on how to approach and review case studies and how to develop focused and highly specific case study answers. In recognition of the fact that coursework is now a key element of many marketing qualifications, advice is also offered on how to prepare and submit case study assignments and practical work-based assignments.

Chapter 9 – Report writing

This chapter offers guidance on how to produce an exam answer or a coursework assignment in the typical 'report format'. The content is designed to assist readers who need to demonstrate the ability to present their findings in the form of a structured professional report.

The report writing principles discussed in this chapter can be applied either in an assessment context, or in a practical work-related situation. The typical sections of a report are summarised and advice is provided on how to present and structure the report.

Chapter 10 – Sample exam questions

A range of intermediate level exam style questions covering a variety of important marketing issues, form the basis of this chapter. However, in order to assist marketing students at every level, guidance is also provided on what examiners are likely to expect from marketing students at the lower, intermediate and higher levels of study.

Chapter 11 – Submission procedure

Because readers have the opportunity to answer and submit the sample exam style questions for marking and feedback, this chapter explains how to submit completed answers for marking by a qualified and experienced examiner. Full details of the submission procedure are provided, including guidance on the required answer formats. Instructions on how to obtain an update on the associated marking fees and turnaround times are also included.

Chapter 12 – Instructional words

This chapter provides an explanation of the meaning of the various *instructional* or *command* words that marketing examiners are likely to use in exam questions.

Additional information about the author

The book concludes with some additional background information for those who may wish to know a little more about the author.

Appendices

Appendix 1 lists the key marketing models that intermediate level marketing students should ensure they are familiar with.

Appendix 2 lists the key marketing topics that intermediate level students need to know about and understand.

Using the remainder of this book

I suggest you begin by making an honest assessment of your personal situation.

Consider the time you have available, your strengths and weaknesses as far as your knowledge of the subject is concerned, plus your recent exam-related experience. Also think about how much time you have available before you must sit the exam, or submit any coursework or work-based assignments.

> **Key Point**
> Aim to be honest with yourself and make an objective assessment of your situation, before deciding exactly how you will take advantage of the information in this guide. Then adopt a reading approach that suits your own particular style, preferences and individual circumstances.

The 2 basic approaches to reading this book outlined in Figure 1.2 are provided purely as a guide.

Ultimately you must adopt a method that is practical and suits you best.

Option 1	Option 2
Work through the whole book or most of the book in a logical progression if........	**Carefully select and prioritise your reading by focusing on a few key chapters if........**
1.You have experienced problems when preparing for exams or when sitting exams in the past. **2.**Your experience of sitting exams is limited. **3.**Your subject knowledge and your practical experience of marketing is limited.	**1.**You have serious time pressures. **2.**You have acquired this book just before you need to sit the exam. **3.**You are an experienced exam candidate just looking for some improvement in certain key areas.

Figure 1.2 The 2 basic approaches to reading this book

If your experience of sitting professional exams is limited, or you have encountered problems in past exams, I recommend you work through this book from cover to cover. If you are faced with serious time pressures, perhaps because you have acquired this book just before you need to sit the exam, you will need to carefully select and prioritise your reading.

Receiving feedback on your performance

Answering questions, then receiving professional feedback on your performance and clear guidance on how your answers could have been improved is an important and worthwhile procedure. If you undergo such a process, it should give you the edge you need when it comes to sitting the actual exam.

You can answer one or more of the set exam style questions included within this book and submit them for marking and feedback if you wish. Once received, your answers to the selected questions will be marked by a qualified and experienced marker and returned to you.

The feedback you receive will incorporate constructive comments on your performance and where appropriate, guidance on how your answer and overall approach could be improved.

More details about the optional marking and feedback facility can be found in Chapter 11.

Chapter 2 – Courses and study methods

The guidance in this chapter is likely to be of particular interest to those readers who have yet to decide on a particular marketing qualification, a specific delivery centre or study method.

If you have not yet embarked on a study programme, it would be a good idea to reflect on the issues highlighted in Figure 2.1 before you make your decision. If you already have progressed through this stage and your marketing course is up and running, feel free to move on to the next chapter. You can always return to this section before you sign up for any future marketing modules or qualifications.

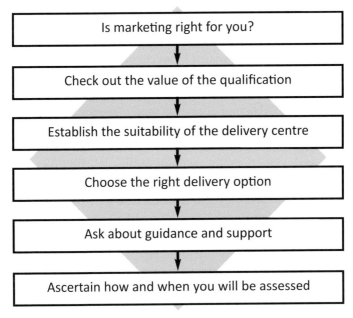

Figure 2.1 Make the right decision

Is marketing right for you?

Let's start by looking at some important factors that ought to be considered by any potential marketing student.

First of all, as with any course of study, you should aim to commit to a study programme that will be both practical and suitable for you. Ideally it should be a course that you will find enjoyable and worthwhile, that also matches your long-term career or life aspirations. If you can, seek objective and professional advice from a few suitably experienced people that you can trust, to help you come to a decision if necessary. Suitable advisors could be qualified marketing practitioners, successful businesspeople, professional educators or career advisors.

If marketing does turn out to be the right subject for you, then conduct some more detailed research on the marketing courses and qualifications that are available. Also check out the delivery centres that run any suitable marketing programmes. Don't forget to find out about the different ways in which you might be able to undertake your particular course of study. Possible study options include traditional face-to-face delivery (involving classes at college or university or intensive residential weekends) or various open, distance or flexible learning methods (online or offline).

Check out the value of the qualification

Don't automatically take the claims made by delivery centre staff, or the statements you have read in any promotional materials for granted. Check up and establish the true credibility and real value of the qualifications. Look for tangible evidence to back up any claims or promises that have been made by certain stakeholders, who may well have a vested interest in signing you up. If it's important to you, ask if the qualifications are recognised worldwide, or if they are highly valued in certain business sectors or industries, such as those you may plan to work in. Why not speak to marketing practitioners or human resource staff in your own organisation, or in the type of organisation you would like to work in the future, to hear what they have to say about how they value a particular qualification or assessment system.

Establish the suitability of the delivery centre

The exam results of most educational institutions are usually freely available. So obtain details of the recent past performance of any potential suppliers such as colleges, universities and distance or online learning providers. Also remember that the people who deliver the programmes are an extremely important component, especially if the programme content is going to be delivered, or supported on a face-to-face basis by a tutor, trainer or lecturer.

The best people to help you achieve success in a marketing exam are those who have practical marketing experience, plus a suitable marketing qualification and a genuine enthusiasm for the subject. Ideally they should also possess a strong desire to develop people, an eye for detail and excellent communication and motivation skills.

Key Point
Don't be afraid to ask about the marketing background and qualifications, plus the teaching experience of the tutor, or tutors who will be working with you. Before you sign up for the course it makes sense to find out a little about the people who will be teaching, tutoring or training you.

If the key issues cannot be communicated clearly and enthusiastically to the students by the tutor, all the experience and qualifications count for nothing.

Like any other employees, tutors change from time to time for various reasons. So ask someone at the delivery centre if the tutor for the forthcoming year is the same person who ran the marketing course on previous occasions.

You may establish that the excellent, very experienced tutor who achieved considerable success at the centre in previous years has just been replaced by a less experienced substitute (or vice versa). While you may not always get the response you hoped for, at least you can weigh up the pros and cons of each delivery centre or study option on an informed basis, before making a final decision.

If you can, try to speak informally with ex-students who attended the same course last year. You could do this at a college open evening, or if you are lucky maybe you will already know some ex-students you could approach for a chat. By doing this you should be able to gain a good indication of the abilities and enthusiasm of the tutor. Remember though, it's a little dangerous to take the word of only one ex-student, just in case that particular individual is biased in some way (either positively or negatively).

In summary, speak to as many people as you can and try to obtain a balanced view about the knowledge, competence, enthusiasm and commitment of the delivery staff.

Choose the right delivery option

Consider what is likely to be the most convenient study method for you, bearing in mind your present circumstances, commitments, lifestyle and preferred learning approach. Various delivery options are likely to be available and making the right choice is crucial.

You may value the discipline imposed upon you by having to make a firm commitment to attend college classes on a regular basis. The opportunity to interact personally with the lecturers and other students in class might be the deciding factor for you.

Alternatively, perhaps because of family commitments, time consuming or costly travel issues, or maybe even your own individual learning style, you might prefer the flexibility and convenience of an open, flexible, distance or online learning approach.

Ask about guidance and support

Find out in advance about the different types of guidance and support that you could drawn on, if needed during your course of study.

It would be helpful to know when and how you can make contact with your tutor if you were to need some extra advice or support. Ask if you can phone or email the tutor, or maybe even call in for a personal chat, if you ever experience any problems or difficulties.

> **Key Point**
> If you can, arrange to meet with the person who will actually be your tutor before you sign up for the course, either at an open evening or during a one-to-one meeting at the educational establishment. While others can discuss the course with you and offer you advice, there is no better person to speak with than the tutor. After all he or she will be the one at the sharp end who will be working with you throughout the study period.

There may well be some specific time set aside for such meetings with your tutor or with any other relevant members of staff, so never be afraid to ask.

Also find out as much as you can about the resources you will be able to access. As indicated in Figure 2.2 these could include libraries and hopefully an up-to-date stock of marketing-related books and suitable marketing, advertising or public relations industry magazines and trade journals. Don't forget to check the opening and closing times of the library and any other facilities you plan to use.

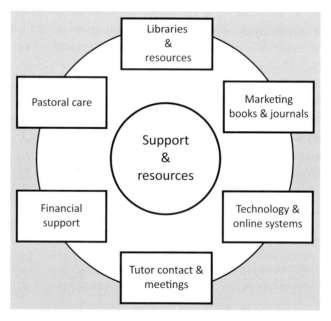

Figure 2.2 Ask about the support and resources

Besides providing academic support and advice, many delivery centres can also support you in various other ways. So don't be shy or embarrassed to ask about what other services may be available to you as a registered student, such as financial support including grants, or the provision of pastoral care if you think it may be needed.

While many academic establishments are currently undergoing changes as a result of financial constraints, never assume there is going to be no financial support available to you. While certain categories of student may have to pay higher tuition fees in the future, others may find their study programmes are subsidised or partially funded depending on individual circumstances.

Don't forget to obtain relevant information on any dedicated online facilities or resources that have been developed specifically for marketing students. The availability and use of information communications technologies means that support and guidance can now often be provided remotely.

Some of these technology-based systems are not all as accessible, simple to use, or as worthwhile as they are sometimes claimed to be. However, many online resources can turn out to be rich and diverse sources of information. They may also provide you with the opportunity to communicate conveniently and effectively with your tutors and fellow students.

If you eventually decide to use any online or other technology-based systems, make sure you keep a careful watch on your time. Chatting aimlessly with fellow students in the 'social' online forum, or posting unnecessary messages is not an efficient use of your valuable time. Such aimless activities are unlikely to contribute much to your understanding of marketing.

If you can, view a practical demonstration of any online support and communications systems that may be available. This should give you a good indication of the possible benefits to you. Demonstrations may occur at a college open evening, or perhaps during a more informal personal visit to the delivery centre.

Be sure to check that you can access the system remotely when you are at home or work, if you must have access to certain technology in order to undertake your chosen study programme.

If access to the Internet or use of a computer outside the delivery centre is mandatory in order to undertake the course, you will need to ensure you have the necessary equipment and a suitable Internet connection. Some delivery centres do lend certain resources to qualifying students for the period of their studies, so feel free to ask about the availability of any loan equipment.

The technical specification and capability of your home computer, the speed of the Internet connection and the associated costs must all be taken into consideration, if you need to access the Internet regularly from home in order to participate fully in your particular study programme. So always ensure you are familiar with the equipment and the type of Internet connection you will need and also how much it will cost you to acquire and run the system.

Ascertain how and when you will be assessed

While the essential exam issues will be addressed in detail later, it's never too early to think about certain exam and coursework matters.

Remember, not all courses and qualifications involve 3 hour formal examinations for each module. So before you sign up for a course, make sure you find out exactly how and when your knowledge and understanding will be tested.

Consider whether you would prefer to sit exams or undertake coursework and the pros and cons of each system. Some certified professional marketing qualifications include a combination of both forms of assessment. In such circumstances you may be required to sit 2 formal exams and also submit 2 coursework assignments (the latter may need to be work-based).

Apart from your own personal preference for undertaking one type of assessment method or the other, you should also think about how prospective employers will view your exam-based qualifications, compared to how they perceive any qualifications that can be gained by submitting 100% coursework. Of course in reality you may not actually have the option to choose one particular assessment method or the other, but it's still worth thinking about these issues before you commit yourself.

If you opt for some form of examination based assessment, make sure you find out the exam dates and times, plus the format of your particular exam well in advance. Professional exams often tend to be set for 3 hours and usually demand essay style, or 'report format' answers. Shorter and possibly lower level exams may be set in a multiple choice answer format, requiring candidates to select the correct answer from a number of different options.

Many marketing qualifications now involve the submission of at least some coursework or assignments for assessment. So if you must submit one or more assignments you should establish the submission deadlines and whether your assignments will need to be work-based, or related to a case study.

More about exams, assignments and the associated techniques later!

Studying marketing as a non-marketer

You may be a reader that doesn't plan to study for a 'pure' marketing qualification, or a marketing-related qualification such as e-marketing, marketing in hospitality and tourism, marketing communications, advertising or public relations. You could be one of the many non-marketers who are required to study a single marketing module that forms an element of a different industry qualification (if so, you can still follow much of the guidance provided earlier).

You can conduct some research on the syllabus and on your marketing tutor's background. In such cases it would be a good idea to also ask about any experience the tutor has gained by working in your own industry.

While there are some excellent tutors around, unfortunately not all are experienced, qualified and competent in the subjects they teach. So reading the tutor's biography early on may give you a good indication of the quality and the degree of support you are likely to receive throughout the study programme.

Chapter 3 – Study planning

Before you start your preferred course of study, you will need to think carefully about how you should approach and undertake your study programme.

As a marketing student you will no doubt become familiar with the SWOT analysis. The SWOT is a tool that is usually used to analyse the internal strengths and weaknesses of an organisation and the external opportunities and threats that may exist.

Strengths
(your skills, resources, attitude etc)

Weaknesses
(the lack of resources, skills etc)

Opportunities
(quiet times, visits, events, take photos)

Threats
(distractions, temptations, pressures)

Figure 3.1 The personal SWOT analysis

At the start of your studies it's a good idea to conduct an objective assessment of your own personal strengths and weaknesses. This particular SWOT analysis should be viewed from the study perspective as outlined in Figure 3.1.

Your personal strengths might include the fact that you already have Internet access at home, which can be used for research or other relevant study purposes.

You might also be able to draw on a network of friends or associates who know something about marketing. If so, take full advantage of any such assets or resources when you need information or support during your course of study. You should also develop a strategy to eliminate, or at least minimise any personal weaknesses you have identified. This might involve filling any gaps in your knowledge, or perhaps improving certain personal skills (such as the speed of your reading).

You must also identify and reflect on the external opportunities and threats that may exist. Then take full advantage of any opportunities, like those which could help you to study more effectively. For example, family members or friends you live with may have a hobby or interest that takes them out of the home regularly on a certain evening each week. You could take advantage of this particular opportunity by reading or undertaking any necessary coursework that evening while the house is quiet.

Strategies can also be developed to counter any threats to your studies, such as making the decision to decline certain non-essential social invitations, which if accepted could easily distract you from your regular studies. Sometimes just learning to say 'no' and politely refusing a very tempting but highly distracting night out, is all you need to do to keep on track with your learning programme.

On the subject of tempting social invitations, it is worth emphasising that we all need to relax and enjoy ourselves on our own or with friends and family from time to time.

So make sure you also recognise and respond to the potential threat of actually devoting too much time to your studies and not enough time to relaxing and enjoying yourself. Aim to strike the right balance that will allow you to adopt a disciplined and rigorous approach to your studies, while also maintaining a fit, healthy, rewarding and relaxing social life.

Develop a study plan

Once you decide on a course of study, it's a good idea to develop a plan that will enable you follow the study programme and achieve all the associated objectives.

The learning institution should be able to provide you with the necessary details and resources you require, to plan and manage your own specific study programme. However, just in case sufficient information is not made available to you, a summary of the key points is incorporated within this guide.

Key Point
Once you commence your study programme and start to work on your reading or research at home, it's a good idea to work in 'bite size' blocks. For example, if you spend around 30 minutes reading or researching and then take a break of 5 or 10 minutes before going back to your studies for another 30 minutes or so, you should find it easier to focus and feel less tired than if you worked for an hour without any break. By all means experiment with different approaches to see which system suits you best.

Establish a timetable

One way of keeping yourself on track is to produce a suitable timetable that covers your period of study.

The timetable can be defined in days or weeks to suit your individual circumstances and preferences.

The basic example illustrated in Table 3.1 has been set up a weekly basis and only covers 4 weeks simply for illustration purposes. A full practical version could cover any suitable period, such as a 20 week course of study.

Week	Key topic	Syllabus	Essential reading	
			Main textbook	Other Source
1	Marketing Concept	Section 1	Read chapter 1 of core text	Read chapters 5 & 6 of secondary text
2	Marketing Environment	Section 2	Read chapter 2 of core text	Read marketing journal
3	Marketing Mix	Section 3	Read chapter 3 of core text	Read chapters 8 & 9 of secondary text
4	Marketing Research	Section 4	Read chapter 4 of core text	Read marketing magazine

Table 3.1 Sample weekly study plan

The timetable headings highlight the key topics that must be studied during each study week, starting with week 1. In some cases it might be appropriate for week 1 to be devoted to a review of the learning materials, or to the preparation of a personal development plan depending on the circumstances concerned and the time available.

The key topics in Figure 3.1 have been cross referenced to the appropriate sections of the syllabus and also linked to the essential reading material. The essential reading covered in the study plan has been divided into 2 distinct categories (reading the main course textbook plus any other essential reading). The other essential reading sources are likely to include alternative textbooks, relevant articles in marketing publications, the quality press or trade journals and any suitable online content.

> ### Key Point
> Never underestimate how much pressure you might be subjected to while studying, working and keeping the family happy. Always set aside some time in your busy schedule to relax and get some exercise. Avoiding stress is an essential part of modern life, so make sure your timetable regularly incorporates some slots that will enable you to chill out in the way that pleases and relaxes you most. I regularly take time out to exercise and walk in the countryside. That means I can rest my brain and get some exercise and fresh air at the same time.

Your timetable can be as detailed as you want and could include estimated timings, plus a column to tick when the various tasks have been completed.

The system you establish should be easy to use and it must allow you to see at a glance exactly what needs to be done each day, or each week. Adding a column or box that can be ticked also provides you with a useful visual indication of your progress (or lack of progress).

Some students prefer to plan ahead on a day by day basis each week, in which case the format shown in Table 3.2 could be used.

Day	Task	Time to be Allocated
Monday	Research set assignment	1 hour
Tuesday	Undertake essential reading	1 hour
Wednesday	Undertake essential reading	1 hour
Thursday	Attend evening classes at college	3 hours
Friday	Undertake review and self-test	1 hour

Table 3.2 Sample 5 day study plan

The example plans illustrated in Tables 3.1 and 3.2 could be adapted for use in relation to any form of full-time or part-time study.

Establishing a realistic timetable will help you to keep on track throughout your course of study. Timetabling is a key component of your study plan. Apart from allowing you to plan and undertake your reading, your timetable can also be used to schedule any assignment or coursework submission dates and of course your revision and exam preparation activities.

Manage and allocate time

Start your studies as you mean to go on by managing and allocating your time effectively. The application of suitable time management techniques will help to ensure that you always devote sufficient time to your studies, without adversely affecting your work or social life.

Begin by establishing the overall time that should be allocated to your studies. Then you can develop a plan to help you manage your time throughout the course of study, including the revision and exam preparation period prior to the exam.

If you are attending classes you may find that each module will involve 30 hours of classroom contact time, which could mean the programme content is delivered in 1.5 hour sessions over 20 weeks. Remember that in such cases, in addition to allocating 1.5 hours per week for classroom sessions, you also need to factor in the time needed to travel to and from the delivery centre.

Each module may require you to spend between 8 and 10 hours per week reading and studying outside of the set classroom hours. So there may be a need for an additional time commitment of give or take 2 hours a day. Obviously your own particular course of study may well require a higher or lower commitment as far as time is concerned, but don't let the time commitment aspect come as a surprise. Make sure that even before you sign up for the course you know exactly what is expected of you and the likely demands on your time over the period concerned.

Tutors should be able to provide students with guidance and a realistic indication of the study hours that need to be allocated in addition to any time spent in face-to-face classroom sessions. So consult the staff at the delivery centre, or contact the awarding body for the necessary details.

All the timings you are likely to be given will be estimates. The actual hours you spend studying will depend on various factors, such as your current level of knowledge and understanding, plus the time you spend accessing or utilising resources and so on. Remember that your overall study time includes the time that needs to be spent in class, the time reading around the subject and time that must be allocated to completing necessary activities or assignments, if applicable.

Some exam or assignment-related focus is also clearly required at the appropriate stage. That means as you progress towards the exam or the assignment submission date, you will also need to acquaint yourself with the key areas that are likely to be examined or assessed. Building in sufficient time for exam revision is essential, so where possible again take advice from your tutor. Don't worry though, you will find a lot more exam and assignment-specific advice in the remaining chapters of this book.

Time management techniques

Once you have considered all the issues and determined how much time you will need to allocate to your studies, try to follow a few simple guidelines that can help you manage and allocate your time effectively.

The example study plans illustrated in Tables 3.1 and 3.2 can also be used to help you manage your study time. As indicated earlier they can be adapted to suit your needs. The headings can incorporate references to timings and 'tick box' sections or columns can be added, so that you can see at a glance what has been done and what is outstanding.

However, the study plan in the form already described only relates to your study time. Therefore you also need to consider how you can successfully manage and effectively utilise the remainder of your time. Some people prefer to keep their study plans completely separate from any non-study time management systems, while others like the idea of combining the two. It's for you to decide how much emphasis you give to managing your study and non-study time, but remember that all your time is important. When you are studying and you also have important work and personal commitments, you can't really afford to waste any time.

If you prefer to separate your non-study time from your study-time, aim to establish a simple standalone system to help you manage the considerable time you spend on your non-studying activities.

Establish a diary or 'to do' list

For general time management purposes it's a good idea to establish a simple system such as a diary or 'to do' list. You can use paper, computer-based or any suitable portable smart technology depending on your preferences, but make sure the system is easy and quick to use and that the data cannot be easily lost.

Each day decide on the most appropriate order in which you should undertake the selected tasks you must undertake that day. Also come to a decision on what can safely be deferred until a later date. Then decide how long you should spend on each of the tasks you plan to undertake that particular day.

You can produce a list for a day or for a week if you prefer (although I have to say I prefer a daily list). Once a task has been completed it can then be deleted from the list. That will give you a clear picture of what tasks have already been achieved and what still has to be done. New tasks can of course be added as and when necessary.

You may decide to use just one system that integrates your study plan and all your work and social commitments in one. Alternatively you might prefer to keep your study plan separate from the management system that covers your work and social time.

Whatever you do, just make sure you keep your system as simple as possible. By all means adapt the system if and when necessary, but be sure to make a pledge to stick to the grand plan – at least until the exam is over, or the assignment is safely submitted!

Prioritising tasks

Understanding the difference between *urgent* and *important* as demonstrated by Figure 3.2 will help you to prioritise your daily or weekly tasks and save you some valuable time.

PRIORITISING TASKS	URGENT	NOT URGENT
IMPORTANT	This task is time-related and it is also significant so do this first	This task is not time-related but it is significant so you decide
NOT IMPORTANT	This task is not significant but it is time-related so you decide	This task is neither significant nor time-related so do this task last

Figure 3.2 Prioritising tasks

The matrix in Figure 3.2 is based on long established time management principles. Both Professor Stephen R. Covey and US

President Dwight D. Eisenhower have been credited with originating the concept, although the time management matrix was certainly popularised by Covey.

Always remember that anything *urgent* is time-related.

When a task is *urgent* it demands your immediate attention. The urgency of a matter is affected by the passage of time.

When a task is *important* it has a high degree of significance. The importance of a matter is not affected by the passage of time.

So when a task is both *urgent* and *important* you need to give it a high priority as indicated in Figure 3.2 and place it at the top or close to the top of your list. Conversely when a task is neither *urgent* nor *important*, it can be given a relatively low priority and placed at the bottom, or towards the end of your 'to do' list.

Of course in reality people have different views about what is important to them, so the prioritisation of tasks is ultimately an individual decision.

Any time you do save by employing time management techniques can of course be devoted to your studies, or to the other areas of your life that are important to you.

Establish a reading file

In addition to reading recommended textbooks and other learning materials, good students make the effort to read relevant articles in carefully selected magazines or journals and the quality press. Many keen students also use the Internet and other resources to gather information about the subject they are studying.

Most marketing exams above the basic or introductory level demand that students convey some knowledge and understanding of current thinking. Reading the latest marketing-related articles and reports is therefore an excellent way to keep up-to-date with current thinking in the particularly dynamic field of marketing.

When you identify any suitable reading material such as magazine or journal articles, make sure you store them appropriately, so you can easily find and review them when necessary. There is usually no need to retain and store the whole publication, so just retain the important sections for more detailed analysis or future reference.

Key Point

Look out for the following marketing industry trade publications as these and others like them contain plenty of useful information and examples:

- '**Advertising Age**' – diverse advertising and marketing resource including online content and email newsletters;
- '**Adweek**' – the latest advertising news for advertising professionals includes online forums and networking;
- '**Campaign**' - weekly trade magazine for the advertising, media and communications industry focusing on breaking campaigns, creative work, news, gossip and analysis;
- '**Marketing**' – weekly magazine for the marketing industry covering media, branding, direct marketing and retail, incorporates news, industry analysis and in-depth reports;
- '**PR Week**' – weekly analysis of campaigns and trends, plus articles and reports involving the world of Public Relations.

Your employer may subscribe to some of these trade magazines. You can also find them in certain libraries or online.

Assuming you have the right to do so, because you have purchased or otherwise legally acquired the material, remove any suitable pages from magazines, journals or newspapers, index them appropriately (such as by subject or A-Z to suit your needs) and then store them in a reading file. You can then access and review the materials at the appropriate time (such as during your revision period prior to the exam).

Traditional paper files are easy to set up and access, provided you have the room for them. If you don't have a folder or a filing cabinet at home with sufficient space, then storing the information electronically is also a good option. Using a computer to store electronic files is likely to save some physical space, and of course it also allows the original magazine or newspaper pages to be recycled in line with current environmental trends.

Storing carefully selected material appropriately and systematically can save you a lot of time. However, make sure you are not breaching copyright and always comply with any relevant rules, laws or regulations that may apply to any of the material you plan to copy and store.

Self-help groups and 'study buddies'

Once you begin your studies there is no doubt you will be faced with various challenges and pressures. That's simply the way it is – 'no pain no gain'.

However, it must also be said that studying can be extremely enjoyable. It may even become somewhat addictive, especially after you begin to achieve some examination successes! Studying opens our minds to new ideas and possibilities and it can sometimes enable us to establish valuable new contacts. If we are really lucky, it might even provide us with the opportunity to make some new life-long friends.

While your future success is in your own hands, don't think you must always undertake your studies in isolation. Besides the valuable relationship you can establish with your tutor, you can also benefit considerably from working with your fellow students.

When I tutor distance learning students, I encourage them to establish self-help support groups. I know from experience that students can benefit at various levels from interacting with each other, while both obtaining and providing peer support.

Key Point
Why not consider how you can link up with other students in your own particular study group. It may provide you with the extra discipline and incentive you need to remain positive and keep on track. It's up to you whether you prefer to work with other students in a small group, or with just one other 'study buddy'. If you eventually decide that linking up with other students is not for you – well that's OK too!

I have tutored mixed groups of distance learning students located in different parts of the UK and also in Africa and South East Asia. These students can't attend a conventional face-to-face class and because of their wide geographical spread, there is a danger individual students might feel isolated.

To help reduce the negative effects that can be associated with this type of remote studying, I provide an opportunity for my students to make contact with each other. Those who are interested and who give permission for their contact details to be circulated are then able to communicate with their fellow students via email. That gives them the opportunity to share their thoughts and concerns, as well as their ideas and points of view with like-minded people who become 'study buddies'. Some students now use 'Skype', which enables them to make free personal and group video calls.

Students occasionally prefer to discuss certain issues with their peers, rather than raising them with the tutor. Some types of student-to-student interaction can be extremely beneficial and can often complement the support provided by tutors (as long as it does not involve any form of collusion or plagiarism if coursework is involved).

Of course today more than ever we all need to exercise caution when it comes to meeting or communicating with people we don't know. We also have to be careful about the nature and level of personal details and contact information we pass on to others. If you find yourself in this situation I suggest you apply normal basic common sense.

After work when I'm in the Middle East I occasionally encounter some of my Kuwaiti students in Starbucks or similar local coffee shops. Because the population of Kuwait is quite small, it's common to meet people you know in the shopping malls and other popular venues.

The Kuwaiti students tend to meet up with their course colleagues at a suitable location, where they can socialise and talk openly without any concerns prior to their marketing exams. Typically in small groups they spend an evening or two going through what they decide are the key elements of the syllabus. They take their pre-exam revision very seriously and in addition to using their personal laptop computers to refer to the course slides, they also tend to produce their own information fact sheets.

These information sheets are circulated within the particular study group following some appropriate group discussion. The resulting fact sheets contain what the student group thinks are the 'hot topics' based on the notes they have taken in class, the experience of some group members and any other information they have obtained.

Provided it's established and undertaken properly, a 'study buddy' relationship or a self-help group such as this can be extremely rewarding and worthwhile for the participants.

However, this type of approach is not right for every student. As already indicated participants do need to exercise the necessary caution and care when exchanging contact information and when meeting new people (especially in the evenings, or when it's on a semi-social basis). In such cases it's advisable to meet in an open and safe social environment, at least on the first few occasions.

> **Warning**
> Meeting people alone in private homes or at offices late at night for study purposes carries a higher risk, so the necessary caution must be exercised. If you are in any doubt whatsoever about meeting someone under what may to you be unusual circumstances don't do it.

If you are in any doubt, don't make arrangements to exchange personal information and don't meet anyone (especially if you would be meeting them unaccompanied or late in the evening).

If you have plans to undertake some form of 'study buddy' or group study arrangement, make the details known to your tutor. That will help to ensure any meetings are likely to be safe and meet with the necessary approval. For similar reasons, it must be said that you should view any one-to-one meetings with your tutor outside the learning establishment with a degree of caution.

These last few paragraphs have been included purely to highlight the fact that meeting anyone we don't know in an unsuitable environment does come with a degree of risk. In practice, most of these 'study buddy' arrangements go ahead without any problem.

Know the syllabus

The best way to approach an exam or assignment is to familiarise yourself with the syllabus, so that you fully understand and appreciate the depth and breadth of the subject.

As soon as possible you should obtain a detailed breakdown of the syllabus and acquaint yourself with the content, including the associated learning outcomes and objectives. You must also identify the various subject weightings, as these percentages indicate the emphasis given to each individual topic and therefore highlight the importance of each element of the syllabus.

For illustration purposes, if the weighting for a topic such as the marketing mix is 25% then this topic is important. It accounts for a quarter of the whole syllabus, so arguably that means 25% of your time should be allocated to studying the marketing mix.

Always adopt a logical approach to analysing and then studying the topics outlined in the syllabus and pay attention to the associated weightings.

However, try not to become too fixated on the numbers. Your aim should be to gain a sound knowledge of the syllabus and a clear understanding of how the key theories and tools relate to the real world. If you are concerned about the syllabus content and weightings talk to your tutor, get hold of some recent past papers and read the latest examiners reports to ascertain exactly what you must know and understand.

Chapter 4 – Effective studying

Most of the guidance in this chapter is applicable to every marketing student.

However, the first 2 sections are aimed specifically at students who receive any form of face-to-face tuition, because they need to undertake certain important tasks such as taking notes.

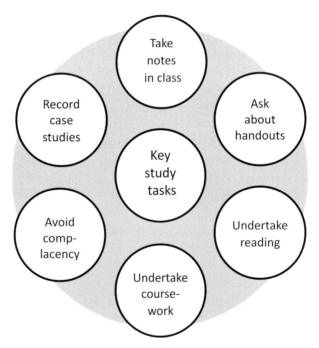

Figure 4.1 Key study tasks

Take relevant notes in class

If you attend classes you need to take full advantage of the advice provided by your marketing tutor. One recommendation that tutors are likely to make is that you should take suitable notes in class.

Taking notes doesn't mean trying to write down everything you hear in class – that's simply not possible for most people. Even if you can write in shorthand, you shouldn't attempt to write all the content of a classroom session or lecture down on paper. While you're focusing on getting everything down on paper, you are not actually absorbing the key points that are being made by the tutor. You may also miss out on some useful and interesting classroom discussions and debates which are likely to occur.

It's best to listen carefully and when a key point is made, note it down in a format that enables you to record it quickly. Remember you will need to interpret it again later in a few months time before the exam, so always write your notes as legibly as you can. Diagrams and bullet points are valuable tools that can be used and integrated within your notes, both to save time and also to help you remember the key points.

If you miss a classroom session ask one or more of your fellow students if you can take a look at their notes (preferably those you have identified as being good students and note takers). While the notes are likely to reflect someone else's views on what was deemed important in the session, if they have been taken carefully they should provide a good indication of what was covered. It ought not to take you long to produce your own version of the key points from somebody else's notes (provided they are structured and clear).

Occasionally a student will ask a tutor if it's permissible to record the sessions or lectures. Some tutors may agree to this and some may not, but you should always ask for permission before you start to record anything. Recording a lecture without the authority of the speaker is not acceptable.

In my personal opinion a recording of a full lecture or training session is likely to be far too broad to be of value. Spending hours listening to a recording of the whole session is simply not an intelligent or profitable use of anyone's time.

The whole point of attending face-to-face sessions is to interact with the tutor and your fellow students and then absorb the key points that are relevant to you as an individual.

> **Key Point**
> Always take your own brief written notes during a class or workshop. You should listen carefully and then identify what you feel are the key points you need to remember. If they are focused and structured, your notes will serve as a useful reminder when you return to them just before you sit the exam, or submit your assignment.

Ask about course handouts

At the start of your course find out if supporting handouts for each session will be circulated to the participants. Handouts could be issued in traditional hard copy format, or they might be made available on a CD, DVD, or even via an online download.

If handouts are available, some tutors may prefer to circulate them at the end of each study session. The argument for this approach is that if handouts are issued at the start of a session, students can become distracted. Some might be tempted to flick through the handouts, rather than listening carefully and focusing on the key points that are being made by the tutor, or discussed by fellow students. After all, the handouts can be read later, but the class may not be repeated until the following academic year!

If any materials are issued at the start of each session, these are likely to be copies of the presentation slides. Hard copies of the presentation slides can be very useful, as they enable students to follow the issues that are being discussed and highlighted by the tutor. Copies of the slides can also be very useful for note taking purposes, because if the tutor expands on a particular topic or makes some important points, students can make suitable notes and comments on, or next to the copies of the appropriate slides.

Some tutors add extra lined sections to their slide-based handouts, so that students can make notes next to the relevant slide.

However, just to be on the safe side you should always take a lined pad and some pens to a class, so that you are self-sufficient as far as your note taking is concerned. Never assume that additional information and note taking resources will always be made available to you.

As many people now use technology-based learning systems it's always a good idea to have a pen and paper available when participating in any online discussions, or when following any suitable podcasts so that you can record any important points.

Learn how you can save a copy of the text-based dialogue that you or other students might have with a tutor during a particularly important online group discussion. Some of these systems have 'save' buttons, but you can also usually highlight the discussion text and then paste it into a word-processing document, so that it can be saved and stored on computer for future reference.

Undertake the necessary reading

An important part of any course of study is the appropriate reading of *essential* and *recommended* learning materials.

In theory, you might imagine that the faster you read the more material you will cover. But remember skipping through the text quickly does involve some risk. Unless you have already developed sound speed reading skills, you might not absorb enough of the key information or essential material that you ideally need to retain.

Sufficient reading time should always be built into your study plan. Always remember that you will need to undertake any *essential* reading that has been specified (because frankly if it is designated '*essential*' this means you must do it). The *essential* reading material will address key areas of the syllabus, so don't ignore it.

Also aim to undertake as much *recommended* reading as possible.

> **Key Point**
> Always read the specified material carefully and selectively. Bear the syllabus weightings in mind when you are deciding what material you should read. Then allocate an appropriate amount of reading time to each important syllabus topic.

At this stage, I feel bound to say that studying any subject is not just about passing the relevant exams or coursework assessments.

The successful practitioners of any discipline or profession are usually also enthusiastic readers and keen observers of what goes on in their particular field of interest within the real world. Reading allows you to see the wider picture, so you can understand and appreciate differing views. It also enables you to gain some knowledge and understanding of how the theory is actually applied in practice.

Undertake the coursework

You may be required to undertake work-based assignments, exercises, coursework or even homework as part of your marketing study programme.

If you are required to undertake any assignments or coursework outside the classroom, make every effort to complete whatever is required and submit the material on time. The coursework topics are likely to relate to important syllabus areas, so you will be adding to your knowledge as you work through the assignments. When you undertake written coursework you will also gain some valuable practice in presenting and communicating your answers on paper.

Know your level and avoid complacency

You can study marketing at any stage from introductory certificate to postgraduate level.

Just like when learning to play a musical instrument, you should join a marketing programme at a stage that matches your current situation and level, while also ensuring the path you take will allow you to fulfil your ambitions. Joining a programme that is too easy will waste your time and probably frustrate you, while embarking on a course that is too advanced for you may present more challenges than you can handle.

> **Warning**
> Never take any course of study for granted, irrespective of your current knowledge, experience and capabilities. By all means be confident, but avoid becoming over-confident or falling into the trap of allowing complacency to set in. Otherwise you might develop a false impression of your true capability.

Aiming to climb the academic ladder quickly is commendable, but taking too many steps before you are ready for them could mean you will lack the necessary grounding in the subject. So take advice from tutors, career advisors, ex-students and professional marketers, before deciding which particular level of study is right for you.

360 degree marketing

Whether we like it or not, we are all surrounded by marketing activities. Most of us are the targets of numerous marketing communications sent through an expanding number of channels, such as those identified in Figure 4.2.

Consumers and businesses are bombarded with all these different marketing messages several times a day. Many of the customer targets are also frequently presented with various product and service offerings.

Depending on your situation, you may feel that such a bombardment of messages and offerings is either good or bad. However, because it is really important for you to gather relevant, contemporary marketing examples that can be incorporated in your coursework or exam answers, at least for now I suggest you regard this virtual marketing avalanche as a considerable bonus.

It means that you don't have to look very far to find some worthwhile marketing examples that can enhance your answers and gain you some precious extra marks!

We'll discuss how to integrate suitable examples within your exam answers later. For now the important thing to remember is that you must make sure you take full advantage of the numerous marketing examples that present themselves each and every day.

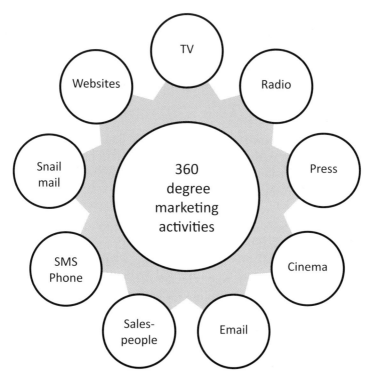

Figure 4.2 The 360 degree marketing bombardment

Record your own case studies

Even the most efficient and organised among us will occasionally forget some of the really good marketing-related examples, because of the many other priorities and distractions we must constantly wrestle with on a daily basis.

To make sure you remember these examples, make a note of the best ones as soon as you see them. These will become your own personal case studies that should easily come to mind when examples are needed in the exam.

When you identify a suitable example briefly note the important details, either by using a few key words or bullet points, or by drawing a basic diagram. The important details can be written out in full later if necessary and placed within the relevant 'example' or 'case study' section of an exam folder created specifically for this purpose.

Creating an electronic record or a paper file that contains your own personal bank of case studies and examples will provide you with a very useful resource that can be consulted when necessary, especially just prior to the exam.

While leaving the bulk of your exam revision to the last minute is certainly not recommended, looking through an 'example' file is one task that can even be left until the night before the exam (if it is absolutely necessary). Any relevant details should then be easy to recall, if the opportunity arises for you to include an example in the exam.

Of course if you have the necessary equipment you can also record selected TV advertisements and documentaries that contain useful marketing examples. These video recordings can be extremely memorable - but don't get too carried away, otherwise you won't have the time to watch them all!

Grab a photo or a short video clip

Small hand-held digital recording devices (including mobile phones, smart phones and digital cameras) also allow us to easily record any suitable marketing-related examples.

When I'm out and about (in the UK or anywhere) I often see some great examples that I can immediately relate to certain marketing theories or concepts.

In Kuwait I see plenty of billboard advertising, both in the traditional poster form and in the latest high-tech display format. Sales promotions in shopping malls are also very popular in Kuwait. It's easy to photograph these examples and then transfer the digital images to my computer's hard drive, so that I can refer to them later if I get stuck for ideas and I'm looking for some inspiration.

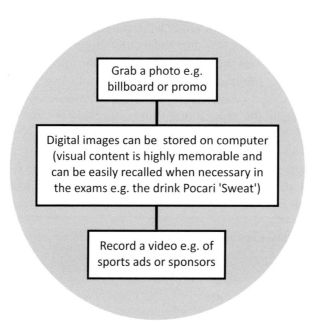

Figure 4.3 Record images and review them before the exam

One photo I took of an Aston Martin car in a shopping mall (part of a Kuwaiti bank's promotional campaign) reminds me that certain types of promotion are more prevalent in particular countries or regions. Billboard advertising and sales promotion is very popular in Kuwait (I have plenty of photos to prove it) while direct mail is not commonly used there, because the postal system is not as it is in the UK or the USA.

On a business trip to Hong Kong I noticed some interestingly named cans in a drinks vending machine. I quickly dug the digital camera out of my pocket and took a photo of the product. It's called Pocari 'Sweat'. The photo reminds me that before attempting to sell an existing product or brand in a new market, marketers should always check the suitability of the product name.

The cans I photographed were being sold in the local Hong Kong market, so the name was not necessarily a problem there. By the way, I'm not criticising the manufacturer of the drinks, it's just that encountering 'sweat in a can' for sale in a drinks vending machine made an impression on me. It also triggered memories of various other similar name-related marketing examples.

If I had to sit an exam now, I could easily remember and then integrate the 'Sweat' example in a suitable answer on the subject of international marketing, branding or new product development.

Key Point

If you have some basic photographic or video equipment (which is now incorporated within most mobile phones) try to capture any interesting or relevant marketing examples that you observe or encounter. You can then take another look at the images to refresh your memory before you sit your exam.

One day you may find a great example of the application of a marketing communications model such as AIDA. If so, take a photo and transfer the image to your computer's hard drive. Make some brief supporting notes as well if necessary and then file them for review prior to the exam.

Warning

Remember that there are certain circumstances under which you should not take any photographs or videos, or when you must at least obtain permission to do. If in doubt don't attempt to capture any image if you feel it might upset anyone, or contravene any local laws or regulations.

If you find yourself in a situation or environment where taking a photograph might cause a problem, let common sense prevail and allow the particular circumstances to direct your actions.

Chapter 5 – Exam preparation

If you have followed the advice provided in the earlier chapters, you should be well placed to face any challenges that may be posed by the exam.

When preparing for the exam, listen carefully to any specific advice given by your tutor if you have one. Also follow the examination guidelines provided by the awarding body concerned. Always aim to undertake the necessary revision and exam preparation within the recommended timeframe and ensure you allocate sufficient time to fully address this important task.

The time you will need to allocate for revision between the end of the course and the date of the exam will vary. However, typically it's measured in weeks, rather than months depending on the various factors involved.

Too little revision too late is clearly a high risk strategy and obviously not a good idea. However, I guess some revision even if it is limited, is likely to be better than no revision at all.

> **Warning**
> If you start analysing past papers on your own too early, you will almost certainly encounter questions on subjects you have not yet explored on the course. This could come as a shock and it might have a negative effect on your confidence, even destroying some of the good work you have already done. So be aware of the dangers associated with taking a look at too many past questions without the support of a tutor, before you have completed the full study programme.

The key stages and issues in exam preparation are set out in Figure 5.1.

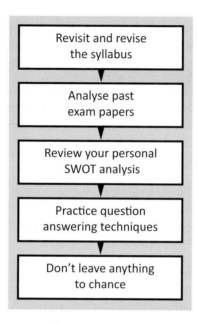

Figure 5.1 The stages and issues in exam preparation

Revisit and revise the syllabus

Begin your revision and exam preparation by re-familiarising yourself with the course syllabus documents and reading list, to ensure you have not missed anything. Then conduct a thorough revision of the topics.

Remember, in the exam you will need to demonstrate that you possess the knowledge and understanding required to meet the learning objectives identified in the syllabus statements.

The relevant marketing theory will often need to be supported by the incorporation of contemporary and appropriate examples.

> **Key Point**
> You must also meet the learning outcomes and provide evidence that you can use a variety of tools, concepts, frameworks and formats. Simply becoming familiar with the nature and purpose of a range of relevant marketing tools and concepts is not enough. At the intermediate level and above, you need to demonstrate the ability to apply tools and concepts in various different contexts.

To make sure you can accomplish all the learning objectives, familiarise yourself with the various assessment criteria you must meet to achieve the grade you require. Your marketing institute or examining body should be able to make this type of information available to you, because your exam answers will be assessed and marked against these criteria.

By the way, check that you are working from the latest version of the syllabus statement and that all your other course-related documentation is up-to-date.

Analyse past exam papers

Awarding bodies can usually provide registered students with examples of specimen and past exam papers. So once the main study programme has been completed, acquire as many copies of the various recent exam papers as you possibly can.

Some awarding bodies allow registered students to download free copies of past papers from the official website. Other institutes sometimes charge a small fee for past exam papers, although your tutor may be able to issue copies for free. If your only option is to pay for past papers, you could consider sharing the cost of acquiring them with some of your fellow students. If you're lucky and you have an experienced and conscientious tutor, he or she might present you with a break-down of some of the relevant, recent past papers at the start of your revision period.

If you don't have a tutor, or if your tutor doesn't analyse the content of past papers for you, you can easily do it yourself. In case you think breaking down the content of past papers may not be an efficient use of your time, I can assure you that any time spent on an analysis of this nature is rarely wasted. In fact it can be highly informative and extremely enlightening.

Key Point

A simple analysis of the questions that have been asked in past papers can highlight important and potentially 'hot' areas of the syllabus that crop up on a regular basis. It might also identify some gaps, such as a few important syllabus areas that so far have not yet been tested (perhaps this could suggest these previously ignored topics might well be due for coverage in forthcoming exams). However, no exam analysis comes with a 100% guarantee!

Of course you can never be sure what will crop up in future exams and making too many assumptions about what might appear in your next exam can be dangerous. Thinking that an analysis of past questions alone will be enough to get you through the exam is a little like playing examination roulette!

Always remember that in an ideal world your aim should be to become familiar with every topic that is covered within the syllabus document. The exam analysis is purely an attempt to fine-tune your preparation and focus your mind during the revision period.

All you need to do to analyse past exam question papers is to produce a simple table that allows you to plot the main subjects that have been tested in the exams over recent years. Once the topics tested in previous exam papers are examined trends may emerge (perhaps indicating that a certain model or concept is very popular or that a particular syllabus element is covered on a broadly cyclical basis).

An analysis of the content of past exam papers is illustrated in Table 5.1.

Exam	Syllabus elements covered				
	7Ps	Coms	MR	NPD	PLC
May 2008	√		√		
Nov 2008		√			√
May 2009			√		
Nov 2009					
May 2010			√		√
Nov 2010		√			

Table 5.1 Analysing the content of past exam papers

Table 5.1 illustrates how past exam papers can be analysed in order to highlight the various topics that were examined in each paper. In reality a wider range of syllabus topics would be placed under the 'Syllabus elements covered' heading.

Review your personal SWOT analysis

In Chapter 3 it was recommended that you undertook a personal SWOT analysis at the start of your study programme.

When you start to prepare for the exam it's a good idea to briefly review and then update your own personal SWOT analysis, because the situation will have changed. This time you should focus on your current strengths and weaknesses and especially on your weaknesses. If any significant or obvious weaknesses are identified, you must make every effort to eliminate them before you sit the exam.

If you still have difficulty with a marketing model or tool that has been identified as a key syllabus topic, then do what you can to clarify the situation by talking to your tutor and/or reading around the subject.

If you can't draw on tutorial support and your reading resources are limited, why not instigate an Internet search on any topics that you may still be unsure about. If you have online access you will no doubt know what Google and other search engines can do for you. So 'Google' any terms or models you need to know more about.

While certain online information sources may be questionable, plenty of reliable marketing-related online resources do exist. Always consult as many online sources as possible to gain a balanced view on any given subject. Then make short notes or draw diagrams to record the key points, so they can be easily accessed and reviewed when required.

Practice question answering techniques

Let's assume you have undertaken a thorough revision of the topics identified in the syllabus and established a sound knowledge and understanding of the subject.

Even though you may have been a model student so far, you could well still have some difficulty interpreting and answering exam style questions. If so, all your earlier efforts could be wasted if you mess up in the exam.

Key Point
Your pre-exam efforts will only count if they are matched by a similar degree of professionalism and commitment in the exam room. Therefore you must practice your question analysis and question answering techniques, as well as your answer planning and answer writing skills.

Before the examination aim to answer as many exam style questions as possible. When your answers are marked and returned to you, carefully read and reflect on any guidance provided by the feedback writer. By doing all this you will put yourself in the best position to obtain a good grade.

Further advice on what you must do to make a positive impression on the marker and maximise your marks in the exam is provided in Chapter 6.

Don't leave anything to chance

Remember that Murphy's Law is likely to apply at some stage, especially on or just before exam day.

Basically this means 'anything that can happen will happen'. To reduce the chances of Murphy's Law coming into play and ruining your exam experience, you must adopt a professional and planned approach in the run-up to the exam.

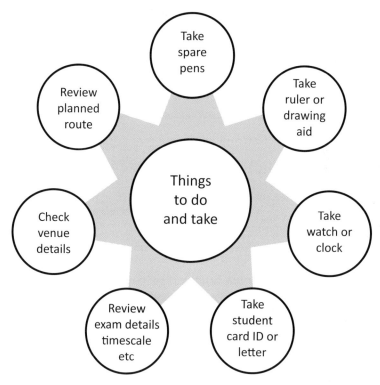

Figure 5.2 Important things to do and take with you

Figure 5.2 identifies the important things to do and take with you to the exam. The night before the exam after reviewing the key topics and reminding yourself of the fundamental examination techniques, pack all the necessary equipment you will need. Include plenty of spare pens, a ruler and any other allowable tools you might need to help you draw straight or curved lines (remember that exam answers often benefit from the use of well drawn and presented diagrams).

Also take any necessary documentation that incorporates your student number and will grant you access to the exam room (such as a student registration card or a suitable official letter). It's possible that you will be required to provide photographic identification to the invigilator along with a current student membership card. A passport, driving licence or ID card may be an acceptable photographic ID, so make sure you pack the relevant ID and take it with you on the day.

Warning
Never assume there will be an easily visible, accurate and functioning clock in the exam room. Always take a reliable watch or clock of your own with you, so that you can monitor and manage the time yourself. You may be used to checking the time by looking at the clock on your mobile phone, but remember you will not be able to access your phone in the exam room!

Don't leave this important final part of your preparation until the day of the exams, because as mentioned earlier Murphy's Law can and often does come into play. You certainly don't want any last minute problems to arise on the morning of the exam.

Remind yourself of the duration of your particular exam – are you 100% sure it is a 3 hour examination? Also ensure that you know the exam format – will some questions be mandatory and others optional? Of course these various factors will depend on the requirements of your exam board.

Double-check the exam venue details, including the room number as well as the name of the building if necessary (don't just assume the site or postal address will be sufficient). Otherwise when you arrive at an unfamiliar location, you may well find you need to waste a lot of your valuable time asking for directions to the correct room or building. Besides wasting time, this would not place you in the best frame of mind to sit an exam. You need to be cool, organised and calm when you enter an exam room (not hot and flustered).

It's also a good idea to check out the best route and how long it should take you to get to the exam venue, considering the time of the day and the day of the week. Remember, sometimes the traffic is especially busy at particular times of the day and on certain days.

Warning
Entry to most exam rooms will be refused 15 minutes after the start of the examination session and you will not be allowed to enter without special permission. Even if you do eventually manage to gain entry, no extra time is likely to be granted.

You don't want to get stuck in a traffic jam because your exam day also happens to be a busy market day, or coincidentally the day when an out of the ordinary event is going to take place. Then all your prior effort and hard work would be wasted. Always allow some extra travel time to account for delays that might be caused by any unforeseen or unexpected circumstances.

Chapter 6 – In the exam

With all the necessary pre-exam preparation completed, please now carefully read and thoroughly apply the guidance in this crucial chapter.

> **Warning**
> If you have not consulted any of the preceding chapters, I would like to emphasise that while exam success ultimately depends on how you actually perform in the exam, there are a lot of things you should do before the exam takes place, if you really want to maximise your marks. Therefore depending on your own particular circumstances and the time you have available, please take a look at the earlier chapters if you can.

The advice that follows is the product of over 20 years successful personal experience of sitting marketing exams, writing exam papers and assessing marketing examination scripts at every level.

As a mature student I learned, refined and successfully applied these crucial exam skills and techniques myself. Later while operating as a marker, feedback writer, senior and chief examiner I developed a sound knowledge and a clear understanding of what a candidate must do to achieve success in a marketing exam.

The guidance in this chapter is based on all of my experiences. I sincerely hope it will also enable you to obtain the examination success that you deserve.

Treat the marker as your customer

If you really want to do well in your marketing exams, besides knowing your subject thoroughly, you must meet the needs of the marker who will actually read and assess your exam script.

Treating markers as customers means giving them exactly what has been asked for in the exam question.

For example, if you are specifically asked to produce an answer in 'report format', then present your answer exactly as instructed. That is precisely what the marker will expect from you and as a reward some additional marks will usually be allocated for suitably presented and structured answers.

Conversely, don't waste time writing out a report style answer, adding introductions, executive summaries, drawing conclusions and making recommendations, if the question doesn't actually call for it. You will simply be wasting your time producing unnecessary content that is unlikely to be rewarded with marks.

Empathise with the marker

Make an effort to empathise with the marker and understand his or her situation. Exam markers are paid a small amount per script and they often have a mountain of exam papers to mark.

This means you really do need to highlight the important issues and communicate the key points effectively, because you cannot be absolutely sure that a particular marker will read and absorb every single word of your script.

I recommend that you view each of your exam answers as an individual product, which must be designed to meet the needs of the marker. The students who develop the most suitable and impressive product portfolio (in this case a suitable number of sound answers) will gain the best marks.

Having made the point that you should empathise with markers and treat them as your customers, it's now time to explore the key tasks that must be undertaken well in the exam.

I know that many students do understand the need to present their written answers clearly and logically. However, experience does suggest that students often don't realise how important it is for them to create a good 'first impression' in the exam.

As Figure 6.1 illustrates, there are 5 essential tasks that need to be completed successfully in the exam.

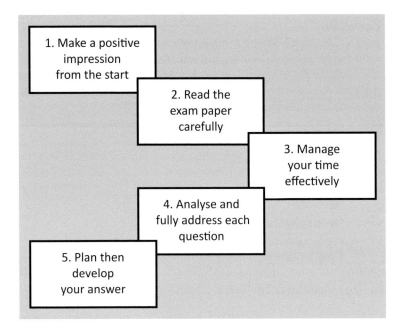

Figure 6.1 The 5 essential exam tasks

Make a positive impression from the start

Your exam scripts must send a positive message to the marker, so you need to take advantage of every opportunity to impress.

Remember that in the exam (as in most other situations in life) you don't get a second chance to make a first impression!

Your exam scripts must always send a positive message to the marker. So make sure that you write as neatly as possible and always complete the exam booklet clearly and fully. That often means inserting the relevant content in the appropriate sections or boxes on the front cover and at the top of each page.

When requested to do so, you must always insert the following:

- your candidate/student number;

- your examination centre number;

- the numbers of the questions you have answered;

- the relevant question number at the top of each page;

- any other details requested by your exam board.

Exam candidates are usually instructed to start their answer to each new question at the top of a fresh page. This approach makes it easy for the marker to differentiate the end of one answer from the start of the next. So make sure you follow these guidelines.

Writing the numbers of each question at the top of the relevant page of the answer booklet also helps to avoid any confusion during the marking process.

Ensure you know all the rules and administrative guidelines in advance, so that you can complete the answer booklet exactly as required in the exam.

Not surprisingly, any unnecessary extra administration can become tiresome for even the most patient marker, who must mark the scripts according to a tight schedule for relatively little financial return.

Even an objective, professional and experienced examiner might subconsciously adopt a negative attitude towards a script that is obviously messy or incomplete. By completing all the sections of the examination paperwork correctly in the exam, you will differentiate yourself from those who may waste a lot of the marker's time because of a lack of care and attention.

Why take the risk of starting off on the wrong note and alienating the marker, when you can send a positive message from the outset by completing the exam booklet neatly and properly.

Read the exam paper carefully

As soon as you are told you can turn over the paper at the start of the exam, make sure you resist the temptation to rush in too quickly and start writing down the answers immediately.

You need to create some clear thinking time before you actually start answering the questions.

At the start of a 3 hour exam you should allocate at least 10 minutes to read and then select the questions you plan to answer. That's a minimum of 10 minutes for reading, reflecting on and selecting <u>all</u> the questions that you plan to answer (not 10 minutes for each and every question).

Manage your time effectively

If you are required to answer optional questions in your exam, always select any optional questions very carefully.

It's best to allocate an equal amount of time to each optional or mandatory question, assuming that all the questions carry the same marks. As illustrated in Figure 6.2 allocating a relevant set amount of time to each question will help you to avoid running out of time at the end of the exam.

If you were to adopt the carefully planned approach illustrated by Figure 6.2, you would have 2 hours and 40 minutes remaining in a 3 hour exam to answer all the questions. That's 32 minutes answering time per question, assuming 5 questions had to be answered and they all carried equal marks.

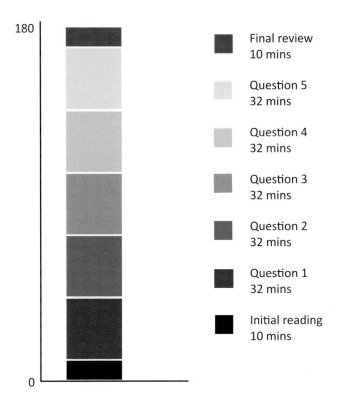

Figure 6.2 Time allocation for a typical 3 hour exam

Having made reference to the marks carried by exam questions, I must highlight the importance of allocating your precious time in relation to the marks available. For example, if 5 questions need to be answered in an exam and they all carry 20% of the marks, then it's logical to allocate a fifth of the 'net time' available to each question. You should always aim to allocate your answering time proportionately.

The 'net time' is what you have left to play with, after setting aside say 10 minutes at the start for the initial reading and a similar amount of time at the end of the exam for a quick final review.

Also be sure to apply the same overall approach to questions that are divided into 2 or more parts. If a 20 mark question is broken down into 2 sections that carry 8 and 12 marks, it's logical to allocate relatively more time to the 12 mark section of the question and relatively less time to the 8 mark section.

Warning

When students get too involved in certain 'attractive' questions, they often leave themselves insufficient time to fully address all the other questions. Make sure you avoid the temptation to spend far too long answering one question, just because you think you know a lot about the topic.

Some exams involve 2 parts, in which case you may be required to answer Part A and Part B. In a 2 part, 3 hour exam you will need to decide in advance how much time you should allocate to Part A which might account for 40% of the marks available and how much time you will allocate to Part B, which may account for 60% of the marks.

Quite a few students run out of time in exams and subsequently receive a fail grade, simply because they didn't manage their time effectively. They get hooked into a question that they like and then spend far too much time on it, leaving them with insufficient time to answer the other questions.

Of course you must make your decision 'on the ground' in the exam, concerning the time you allocate to each question. Just be sure you set yourself clear limits as far as the investment in time and effort on each question is concerned and aim to stick to them whenever possible, unless there is an extremely good reason for not doing so.

The law of diminishing returns

Experience suggests that the law of diminishing returns applies when you answer an exam question.

Warning

In an exam context the law of diminishing returns means that after a certain point in time, the extra marks you are likely to gain are not worth the additional time and effort you are likely to spend on developing the answer further. Therefore to avoid wasting time, it is important to know when to finish answering one question and when to start investing your time and effort in another.

When students become drawn into producing overly long written answers, the first half of the exam answer often tends to be rewarded with more marks than the second half.

Experience does suggest that there comes a point during the production of a particular answer where some students lose concentration, or run short of ideas. In such cases the content in the second half of the answer tends to lack focus, or often duplicates material that was incorporated earlier.

Therefore always ensure that you avoid the potential trap of spending too much time on one answer. Your time may well be spent more profitably on answering other questions, or reviewing any answers you completed earlier in the exam, to see if you can add anything of value that will gain you some additional marks.

Analyse and fully address each question

Occasionally students ignore the question asked and go on to provide an answer that does not address the key points.

Ironically students who sometimes do this may actually have a good knowledge of the subject, but of course that does gain them any marks if they answer their 'own question', rather than the one set by the examiner. Carefully analysing the question, planning the answer and specifically addressing the key issues are all important elements of good exam technique.

Underlining the key words, including any important instructional words contained in the question (such as 'describe', 'explain' or 'evaluate') is a good idea, because it helps to focus your attention on the key issues. Of course, you also must make sure you actually do 'describe', 'explain' or 'evaluate', so that you fully address all the main points.

Underlining the key words is a simple but effective question analysis technique. An example of how to apply this technique in your exam, or in preparation for undertaking any assignments is provided in Chapter 7.

Don't repeat the question in your answer

By the way, don't waste your precious exam time by repeating the question at the start of your answer. Some students do this every time they answer a question, even though it has no value whatsoever. Marks are not awarded for repeating the question.

Adopt the correct format

An exam script should be easy to read and easy to mark.

The style and format of your answer will need to match the type of exam, or the individual topic involved. Occasionally a particular answer style, such as a 'report format' might be specifically requested in the question.

If you are asked to produce an answer in 'report format' you should aim to do so. A simple enough request perhaps, but in an exam students don't always follow simple requests. As a result of not following simple instructions, these students lose out on the valuable presentation marks that are likely to be available.

Whether or not a 'report format' is required, all exam answers will benefit from having a clear beginning, a clear middle and a clear end. That means you should aim to start your answer with a brief introduction, or an explanation of the concept and then develop the remainder of the content in a clear and logical manner.

Incorporate headings and paragraphs

Markers want to read relevant and focussed answers that commence with a suitable concise introduction and then go on to logically and fully address the question.

After the introduction you can use the various headings that may have been identified in your answer plan (see Chapter 7) to help you structure the 'main body' of your answer. If you use short paragraphs with a single line of space between each paragraph (as in this book), you will also improve the chances of the content being identified, absorbed and understood by the examiner.

In many cases it's advisable to conclude an exam answer with a short summary of the key issues covered in the 'main body' (note this final summary should be a concise reminder of the key issues and not a virtual duplication of the full content). The summary is your opportunity to reinforce the key points you have made. If the marker has missed anything important in the 'main body', he or she is more likely to identify it in the final summary.

When a 'report format' is requested, conclusions may need to be drawn in an appropriate 'Conclusions' section. Therefore in such instances a separate summary of the key issues may not be required. Some more detailed guidance on producing an exam answer or an assignment in 'report format' can be found in Chapter 9.

Select your words carefully

Think carefully about the words and phrases that you should use to convey your message effectively to the marker. This may be a further challenge in the heat of the exam, but do your best to remember that the students who communicate their messages and ideas clearly, will probably establish a considerable advantage over those who fail to communicate effectively.

Aim to use the most appropriate words and terms in your answers and by all means convey that you are familiar with the use of relevant marketing terminology.

Certainly use subject-related terms such as 'cognitive dissonance' or 'normative compliance' when there is a suitable opportunity to do so, but always make sure you use them in the right context. Don't repeat your favourite terms in every answer though, as relying on or overusing the same terms may give the impression that your subject knowledge is actually fairly limited!

It's best to keep your message simple and appropriate, because the marker won't have much time to spend reading each answer. Of course the topics and issues you address in your answers may sometimes be complex, but there is no need to make any of your answers too complicated. Place the emphasis on communicating clearly and appropriately, so that your message is more likely to be received and understood by the marker.

If you do run out of ideas in the exam, resist the temptation to fill the empty space on the page with a mass of irrelevant content that doesn't add any value.

Perhaps some students think markers simply award marks based on the volume of words, rather than on the quality of the content. In fact the vast majority of markers recognise this 'padding' for what it is, and consequently they don't reward it with marks. Some exam markers even find the masses of irrelevant 'padding' they sometimes encounter extremely irritating. So any 'padding' in your answers may actually work against you rather than for you!

Simply move on to the next question if you do run out of ideas, or go back and review some of the answers you wrote earlier in the exam.

When you return to some of your earlier answers, you may find that some additional valuable ideas and points have come to mind in the meantime. Any suitable material that you think will add value can then be placed at the end of the appropriate answer (assuming you have remembered to leave some space at the end of each answer for this purpose).

Incorporate diagrams

The appropriate use of diagrams helps you to communicate issues clearly, demonstrate knowledge of a particular tool or concept and save valuable time.

The example diagram in Figure 6.3 is purely a generic 4 box matrix included for illustration purposes. A simple diagram like this can be used as the basis for producing the 'Boston matrix', the 'Ansoff matrix' and various other marketing concepts.

If a picture can be worth a thousand words, then a clear and suitably constructed relevant diagram also has a considerable word count value.

Title

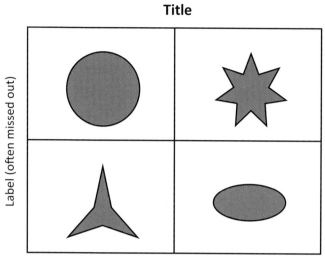

Label (often missed out)

Figure 6.3 Sample diagram of a generic 4 box matrix

Diagrams can often be incorporated to good effect in most exam answers. They can also play a very important role in answer planning during the exam as explained in Chapter 7.

> **Warning**
> Any omissions can cost you dearly in terms of marks. So make sure that when you produce a diagram, you add a title and you also label any axes if it is appropriate to do so. This is a really easy way to gain a few extra marks, but it does emphasise the point that you need to be familiar with every aspect of the models or concepts concerned.

I always encourage marketing students to incorporate suitable diagrams within relevant exam answers for the sound reasons already mentioned. I'm not sure why, but many students appear to ignore this important advice. If they are drawn properly and integrated correctly, diagrams can add considerable value to your exam answers. Of course, when your answers increase in value – so do your marks!

Make use of examples

When you are asked to incorporate relevant examples you must include them, if you want to maximise your marks.

The marks allocated for examples will vary and not every answer will call for them. However, if you don't include an appropriate example when you have been asked to do so, such an omission is likely to cost you quite a few marks.

Warning
Examiners are issued with marking schemes that prescribe how marks should be awarded. When the question demands that examples should be incorporated in the answer, the examiner can only allocate the marks if this particular aspect has been addressed. So leaving out an example can lose you some precious marks (such an omission could result in you gaining a marginal fail instead of a pass, or a pass instead of a higher grade).

While markers may have a degree of flexibility and can sometimes use their discretion and professional judgement when marking, in general they must follow the set marking scheme provided. So if you impress the examiner with some highly relevant and contemporary examples, you should be rewarded accordingly for your efforts.

I can only speak for myself, but on the rare occasion when I see a highly relevant and up-to-date example that hasn't been used by other exam candidates I am suitably impressed. That's because often examples aren't included in answers when they are requested. Even when they are provided they tend to be the same old examples.

Make the 20 exam promises

Discipline is an important quality in an exam, because generally speaking you need to stick to your exam plan. However, flexibility is also a requirement, which means you must be able to change when necessary and adapt appropriately to any unforeseen situations that may arise.

> **Key Point**
> You must think ahead and consider how you will approach the exam, just like a professional sportsperson who visualises exactly how to approach an important game. If you anticipate some potential problems that could occur and think about how you might deal with them in advance, you will be more likely to be able to cope with any difficult situations if they arise in the exam.

The development of a disciplined approach involves making and keeping a few important promises before you enter the examination room and sit the exam. I used to make the following promises to myself and I'm sure if you make and keep them, these 20 exam promises will also work for you.

The first promise is more relevant to the pre-exam issues covered in Chapter 5, but the remainder relate to the actual exam.

1. I will arrive at the exam early just in case of any transport or other unforeseen problems and I will make sure I take all the necessary resources I will need (pens, ruler, watch, student membership or ID card and number, plus any other necessary items or paperwork).

2. I will approach the exam calmly, confidently and professionally and I will not let anything distract me before I enter the examination room.

3. I will spend a few minutes carefully reading the exam paper and

gathering my thoughts (maybe give or take 10 minutes in a 3 hour exam).

4. I will carefully select the most appropriate questions for me to answer.

5. I will manage the remainder of my time effectively so that I don't run out of time, or have too much time to spare at the end of the exam.

6. I will thoroughly analyse each question before I attempt to answer it.

7. I will produce a brief answer plan for each question before I write out my full answer.

8. I will focus specifically on addressing precisely what has been asked.

9. I will ensure that my answer is legible and presented appropriately.

10. I will add spaces between paragraphs to make my answer easier to read.

11. I will incorporate clear and appropriate headings and sub-headings to highlight the key elements and issues that need to be addressed.

12. I will make sure that my answer follows a logical structure.

13. I will incorporate relevant models and diagrams when it is appropriate for me to do so.

14. I will not waste valuable time by covering irrelevant issues that will not gain me any marks.

15. I will resist the temptation to dump masses of totally irrelevant theory or 'padding' into my answer, that does not add value and may frustrate the marker.

16. I will provide relevant contemporary examples where appropriate and especially when I have been specifically asked to do so.

17. I will make a real effort to relate my answers specifically to the scenario or case study (if included) when asked to do so.

18. I will remember that the quality of my answer is more important than the quantity of words I might use.

19. I will remember that thorough answers will gain higher marks than brief answers, as long as I maintain the quality of the content.

20. I will not get distracted by anything while I am sitting the exam and I will remain focused at all times.

There may be some other exam promises you need to make. So why not add some of your own personalised ones to the list, if you think they will be required.

Differentiate your answer

As a marketing student you should be familiar with the concept of differentiation, so aim to differentiate your exam script in a positive way from all the others the marker has to read.

Make sure your answer is well presented, so that it grabs the attention and gains the interest of the marker. You can do this by using appropriate diagrams and highlighting the key issues in a clear and logical manner.

A sound well presented and structured answer that incorporates suitable headings and sub-headings is likely to please the marker. As a result, your marks should reflect the considerable efforts you have made.

> **Key Point**
> Important though it is, of course presentation is not everything. Marketing students at intermediate level should also be familiar with a range of marketing models, tools, concepts, frameworks and topics. The key marketing models and topics that need to be understood are listed in the 'Appendices' section at the end of this book.

Chapter 7 – Answer planning

You won't gain high marks simply by producing an answer plan.

However, if you produce a brief, carefully considered and constructed answer plan and then go on to utilise it appropriately, your full answer is likely to be better than it would have been if you didn't produce a plan.

Why produce an answer plan?

The reasons for producing an answer plan are simple but sound.

Investing just a few minutes in developing an answer plan allows you to reflect on a range of issues and quickly brainstorm possible options and potential approaches.

If it's well constructed, the answer plan (often prepared in the form of a simple diagram) will help you to develop all the key elements clearly and logically in the actual answer. You can think of the answer plan as the template on which the full written answer is based. The key points identified in the plan eventually become the main headings within the full answer.

The end product is likely to be a more appropriate, focused and easier to read answer. Figure 7.1 illustrates the various steps and issues that are involved in the production of an exam answer plan.

You can produce your answer plan on a loose sheet of paper that can subsequently be attached to the full answer with a treasury tag (if that's how your particular exam script should be submitted). Alternatively, you can develop your answer plan within the answer booklet that will be issued in the exam.

To be sure your plan is recognised as such; just add the title 'Answer Plan' at the top of the page.

It's best if you write out your full answer on the pages that immediately follow the relevant answer plan. Placing the plan next to the answer makes it easier for the marker, who then doesn't have to waste time trying to find a plan that may be hidden at the end of your answer booklet.

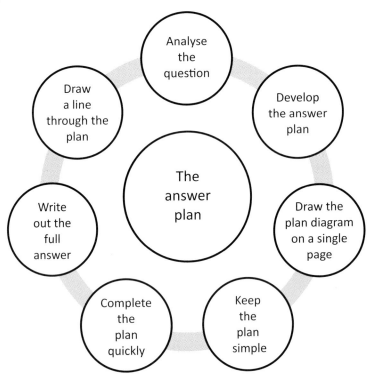

Figure 7.1 The steps and issues involved in answer planning

Always remember that a good answer plan is an investment rather than a waste of time, because more focused, structured and relevant answers are likely to result once the appropriate techniques have been applied.

Sometimes markers may even be able to award extra marks for material contained in the answer plan. A good plan also sends a positive message to the marker about your overall approach, which certainly can't do your cause any harm.

Once your answer has been written out in full, a single diagonal line should be drawn through the plan. This line informs the marker that the material is just your plan and not a part of your final answer. The single line still allows the marker to read the plan without any difficulty.

Warning

Avoid placing all your answer plans together at the end of the answer booklet. If your full written answers don't use up all of the pages in your answer booklet, a marker could assume all the remaining pages are blank. If so, any material placed at the very end of the booklet may be missed. Conscientious markers will flip through every page of an answer booklet including all the blank pages - but frankly you can never be sure that will happen!

Exam scripts that are initially awarded an overall mark just below a pass grade (such as 46 to 49 marks where 50 marks is the pass rate) will usually be given a second look. In fact when a script falls into the marginal fail category after the first marking, marker guidelines tend to state that a review or second marking should be undertaken as a matter of policy. The second marking may be undertaken immediately by the original marker, or it could be done by the senior examiner or another marker.

When reading through all the answers of a marginal exam paper for the second time, markers will carefully review the material.

While the answer plan may not be considered at all during the initial marking (since it's technically not part of the final answer) it's very likely to be reviewed the second time round. This is because markers will be looking for any content that might justify the allocation of a few extra marks (that can turn a marginal fail script into a bare pass).

So if you have prepared an answer plan and your script is marginal, extra marks may well be awarded for certain material contained within your plan, even though it was not actually incorporated in the final answer. Of course if an answer plan doesn't exist, the chances of the marker finding a few extra marks to upgrade a marginal fail grade to a bare pass are reduced.

What does an answer plan look like?

There are no hard and fast rules when it comes to producing an answer plan. However, as identified in Figure 7.2 the key elements of any plan are simplicity, clarity and relevance.

I have seen some good answer plans that have been produced in a 'bullet point' or list format. However, in my opinion a simple diagram is the best way to formulate an answer plan.

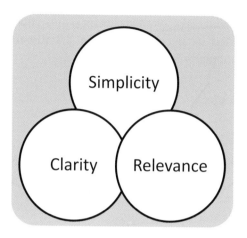

Figure 7.2 The key elements of an answer plan

When I was a student one of my tutors introduced me to the 'spider diagram'. At the time answer planning was a new approach for me, but thankfully I immediately saw the logic and understood the value.

Subsequently many of my own students have also found that drawing a spider diagram like the one in Figure 7.3 helps them to develop highly focused and logically constructed answers.

As can be seen in Figure 7.3 a spider diagram is essentially a simple form of mind map.

To produce a spider diagram you should place the main theme, or core issue raised by the question in a circle (this becomes the body of the spider).

A series of lines can then be drawn in an outward direction from the circle (these lines become the legs of the spider).

The key issues and tasks, or any relevant points you have identified should be added as necessary. Figure 7.4 illustrates how this technique can actually be applied.

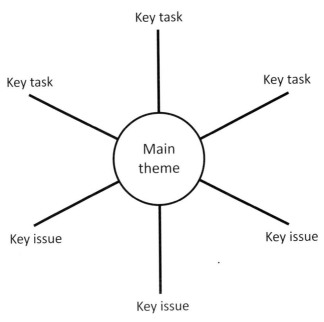

Figure 7.3 The basic spider diagram structure

Various different answer planning techniques exist. So by all means experiment and go with the approach and format that suits you best.

Following a few minutes thought and some focused effort, you should end up with a spider diagram that will provide a useful framework on which to construct your answer.

The resulting answer will be easier to read and far more likely to address the key points that were raised in the question, than if you simply rushed headlong into the answer without thinking carefully about the important issues.

A sample answer plan

The answer planning approach outlined earlier will now be applied to a sample exam style question from Chapter 10.

It is important to remember that no two people will produce exactly the same answer plan. So if you analyse this question yourself and produce a plan of your own, just reflect on any similarities and differences between the example in Figure 7.4 and your version.

Question 1: <u>Discuss</u> what is meant by the term <u>Relationship Marketing</u> and using an appropriate <u>framework</u>, <u>demonstrate</u> how the <u>relationship</u> with a <u>buyer</u> can be successfully <u>developed</u> by the <u>supplier</u>.   (20 marks)

Underlining the key words

The key words in the sample question have been underlined as part of the initial analysis, in order to highlight the important issues. Try to be selective when underlining what you consider to be the most important instructional or content-related words.

Obviously if you aren't careful you will underline everything, which defeats the object of the exercise. Different people may underline different words, but as long as the key issues are identified and highlighted, this approach should help you to focus on the main points that must be fully addressed in the answer.

In this case the words 'discuss' and 'demonstrate' have been underlined because they are important instructional words (they tell you what to do).

Underlining the term 'Relationship Marketing' is important because that has been identified as the main theme of the question.

Underlining the word 'framework' emphasises that a relevant tool or concept must be used.

In this particular example the word 'relationship' has also been underlined, since it relates to the main theme of this answer. However, some students may feel it's not necessary to underline 'relationship', because the 'relationship marketing' issue has already been highlighted.

Finally, highlighting the words 'developed' plus 'buyer' and 'supplier' emphasises that this answer needs to explain how suppliers successfully develop the relationship with buyers.

> **Key Point**
> It's a good idea to discuss question analysis techniques with your tutor if you have one and also with fellow students. Discussions about the important words in a particular question, or debates concerning the pros and cons of any other analysis techniques are likely to be extremely beneficial. If your tutor doesn't raise the subject of question analysis, maybe you could stimulate a class discussion on the subject.

Drawing the diagram

With the key words underlined the initial analysis is complete.

The next step is to formulate the answer plan. This is achieved by producing a spider diagram as illustrated in Figure 7.4.

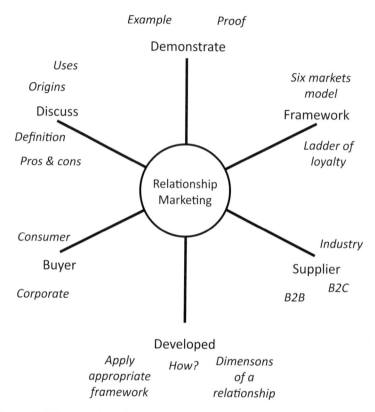

Figure 7.4 A completed answer plan diagram

Start by identifying the main theme

In the completed diagram illustrated in Figure 7.4 the main theme of 'Relationship Marketing' was circled and placed at the centre.

To identify the key issues, attention was paid to the various other words that had been underlined in the analysis.

The single word 'relationship' was not illustrated separately, because it would only have been a duplication of the main theme.

Because it's a key task that must be undertaken, the word 'discuss' formed one leg (the eventual discussion is likely include an examination of the pros and cons using logical argument).

The term 'framework' formed the basis of another leg (as a reminder that the selection of a suitable tool or concept is required). A brief brainstorming of concepts or frameworks could take place on this leg. The most appropriate framework would then be incorporated within the full written answer. In this case either the 'loyalty ladder' or the 'six markets model' are suitable options.

Because this is essentially a two-part question (the analysis actually makes this clear even though it may not be obvious at first glance) the word 'demonstrate' formed the basis of another leg. As it's an instructional word, 'demonstrate' means that you must offer logical proof through the use of an example.

The remaining 3 words that were underlined in the analysis formed the last 3 legs of this particular spider diagram. The 'developed' leg can be used to explore the dimensions of a relationship and how it can be developed. The 'buyer' and 'supplier' legs can be used to identify the most appropriate examples for use in the answer. By highlighting various options it should be easier to identify a suitable example, involving either a B2C or a B2B buyer/supplier relationship.

After reflecting on the issues identified in what has now become the completed answer plan, the structure and content of the full written answer can be developed.

This particular question demands an answer that examines the nature of relationship marketing and then goes on to demonstrate how the relationship between a buyer and a seller can be developed.

As this is a marketing question the answer would need to be written from the supplier perspective, in order to convey how a particular supplier could successfully establish and build the relationship.

The 'loyalty ladder' is an appropriate framework that could be applied in this answer. However, just a theoretical description of the ladder would not be sufficient to gain a good grade.

In order to gain high marks, the answer would need to fully address the 'demonstrate how' aspect, by explaining exactly what the particular supplier would need to do to move the buyer up the relationship ladder. The incorporation of a suitable practical example would also have a positive effect on the overall mark.

Chapter 8 – Case studies and assignments

At some point most marketing students will be expected to address a case study scenario in their exam. Many also need to submit some form of assignment in order to gain their marketing qualification. This chapter offers some advice on how to handle case studies and prepare coursework, including work-based assignments.

Working with case studies

Case studies are often incorporated within intermediate and higher level exams. At the intermediate level they may amount to 1 or 2 pages of text in the exam paper that outlines an organisation and a particular scenario. In an intermediate level marketing exam you might need to answer 2 mandatory questions that relate to the case study. In such cases valuable marks are usually available for applying the relevant theory specifically to the case study, by utilising suitable marketing tools and frameworks.

> **Warning**
> Many students fail to relate their answers specifically to the case study and as a result they lose precious marks. So always read and analyse the case study and make sure you do all you can to link your answer appropriately to the scenario. Remembering to apply your answer to the case study is a fairly easy way to gain valuable additional marks.

At the higher level, case studies may be issued in the form of a multi-page booklet in advance of the exam. Higher level students are required to analyse the substantial case study content (again using suitable marketing tools and frameworks) in preparation for answering the relevant case study questions in the exam.

When working with case studies at any level, you must aim to familiarise yourself with all aspects of the scenario, including the circumstances, organisational and industry issues, any other relevant external or internal factors, plus of course the important marketing issues that are likely to be involved.

As the level of the qualification increases, you must demonstrate that you possess increasingly more sophisticated analysis, planning and communication skills. In addition to fully addressing the key issues raised in the question, higher level answers should be communicated in a suitably professional and competent manner.

Synthesising your thoughts and exercising judgement

When presented with a case study you are required to demonstrate the ability to analyse a particular marketing situation, which will usually be based on a given scenario.

It is also likely that you will be asked to adopt a specified role, such as that of a marketing manager or a marketing consultant. If so, any associated case study questions should be answered in context. This usually means that you will have to draw suitable conclusions and then make some appropriate recommendations, based on your analysis of the situation.

Case studies are an excellent opportunity for you to apply the relevant marketing theory. They allow you to demonstrate your understanding of the issues and your ability to relate the relevant marketing theory and concepts to a given situation. Naturally case studies cannot totally replicate reality, but they do represent the examiners best attempt to simulate real world situations, within the constraints that are imposed by the examination environment.

To handle a case study effectively you will need:

• A sound knowledge of the marketing theories, concepts, tools and frameworks that have been identified in your particular syllabus document;

• A good understanding of how to apply the relevant tools and frameworks and relate the appropriate theory to practice;

• The ability to analyse a particular marketing situation utilising the appropriate tools and frameworks;

• The ability and confidence to make realistic assumptions when necessary (since no case study will contain all the information you require and some may be intentionally or unintentionally vague);

• The ability to synthesise thoughts and crystallise ideas in order that suitable conclusions may be drawn;

• The ability to exercise judgement and critical thinking;

• The ability to adopt a creative and logical approach so that relevant solutions, or recommendations can be proposed;

• An awareness of the role, responsibilities and the expected approach of the particular marketing protagonist that may have been identified in the scenario;

• An appreciation of the key factors and issues that are likely to affect (or prevail within) a given industry, sector or organisation;

• The ability to plan and execute the task in such a way that the analysis and any associated conclusions, or recommendations are related specifically to the case study and scenario;

• The ability to present or sell a point of view and communicate your thoughts and ideas clearly, concisely and effectively.

Case study questions can relate to any topic that has been identified in the syllabus document. So don't assume you will always be asked to conduct an environmental analysis, handle a product launch, or recommend a marketing or promotional strategy.

> **Key Point**
> If you are studying for a certified marketing qualification, you will not usually need any specialised knowledge of a specific industry or a particular business sector, to successfully answer any case study-specific questions. However, if your exam is related to a single module of a non-marketing industry qualification (such as a banking, purchasing, tourism or any other specialised qualification) clearly you are likely to require at least some knowledge and understanding of the particular industry concerned.

Examiners don't expect you to be an expert in everything, but at intermediate level they do expect you to make an effort to establish how marketing actually works in practice.

If you have followed the guidance already provided in this book on the identification and storage of your own examples, you will have already obtained some knowledge and understanding of how marketing is applied in the real world. So draw on your own examples, the case studies provided by your tutor and any others that you discover in your course-related reading.

Make an effort to selectively read suitable marketing and business articles that cover a diverse range of industries from car manufacturing to supermarkets. There is a very good chance you will be able to utilise some of the material in the exam. By reading the appropriate industry-related publications you can familiarise yourself with the marketing strategies or tactics that certain organisations have recently adopted. You may also learn how they have taken advantage of certain opportunities or minimised particular threats. This valuable, specific and up-to-date information can be put to good use in the exam, especially when addressing case study questions.

Just think how convenient it would be if your case study in the exam was based on a motor manufacturer or a supermarket, just a short while after you had read about the activities and also the issues faced by organisations operating in these sectors.

While you would be lucky to see one of your own favourite industry examples crop up in a case study, some of the strategies or tactics you have observed being used in one company or sector might still be applicable to the case study scenario. That's because certain marketing techniques and approaches that are employed by one industry or organisation can also be applied successfully in others (provided all the conditions are right).

> **Warning**
> While it can be beneficial to apply your knowledge of similar organisations or situations to a case study scenario, be very careful that you don't let your prior, or 'inside' knowledge take you down an inappropriate path that leads you away from the main issues. In their enthusiasm to answer a case study question because the scenario appears similar to something they know about, some students become distracted and end up producing an answer that relates to their own example, but not to the actual exam case study.

Even if the case study is not actually based on a particular organisation that you recognise, you can still use your knowledge of a similar business in the same sector to help you analyse the case study scenario and address the question.

Where possible you must base your answer on the information provided within the case study. However, sometimes you may have to make certain assumptions, especially when there is a lack of information or a degree of ambiguity.

> **Key Point**
> While it is permissible to make relevant assumptions when answering case study questions (or any other exam questions), always make a note to that effect at the beginning of your answer. Then your assumptions and your approach can be clearly understood by the marker and any possible confusion can be avoided. Stating your assumptions at the beginning of an answer helps the marker to understand why you adopted your particular approach and as a bonus it may also make a positive impression!

I can't tell you precisely how often students fail to relate their answers to the case study even when specifically asked to do so, but take it from me it happens frequently.

Always remember that precious extra marks are available for the application of relevant theory to the scenario, but markers can't award these additional marks unless they observe the appropriate application of relevant theory.

Time management and the 'double dip' approach

As highlighted in Chapter 6, time is an important factor in exams and during the assignment preparation and submission process.

Because the case studies and any associated case study questions need to be carefully read and fully analysed, effective time management is particularly important when working with case studies.

When tackling a case study some students favour the 'double-dip' approach. This means that initially you should quickly read the relevant case study material and also the associated case study questions.

During this first quick reading you don't need to underline or highlight anything, just gain an initial impression or overview of what is required. Then as your thoughts begin to settle down you should read the case study again, but this time read it more carefully and slowly than you did on the first occasion.

During the second reading you can underline or highlight any key words or important points (those in the case study itself and also in the exam questions that relate to the case study). Try to avoid the temptation to underline or highlight too many words or issues.

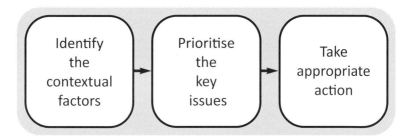

Figure 8.1 The basic case study approach

A useful approach that you can use to help you tackle case studies and answer the associated questions is shown in Figure 8.1.

Identify the contextual factors

When attempting to answer a case study question you must first identify the contextual factors.

These could relate to any key background details, or any relevant data or information you consider to be significant in setting the scene and building a picture about the organisation or its situation. It might be a break-down in sales turnover by product or region, or it might be the number and location of the case study organisation's branches.

Common broad contextual factors include either a domestic, or an international setting, a product or a service supplier, a profit or not-for-profit sector organisation, or a B2C or B2B situation.

Prioritise the key issues

Once the contextual factors have been identified, you need to focus your attention on the important issues and essential tasks. Certain irrelevant issues that may have been mentioned or raised in the case study can possibly be ignored.

You must decide what is important, both from a contextual and from an action or task point of view.

For example, after some careful reading and reflection you might feel that one of the important issues is the B2B context identified in the question. You may also decide the key action or task is the recommendation of a suitable promotional mix.

In order to successfully integrate these 2 key elements correctly and develop the key issues within your answer, you would need to recommend a promotional mix that is relevant to an organisation that operates in a B2B context.

Besides paying attention to all the relevant contextual factors, make sure you also identify all the necessary actions or tasks that you need to perform. Apart from the main task there might be some secondary actions that you need to undertake. A secondary task or action (which is also likely to carry some precious marks) might be the need to produce your answer in a 'report format'.

Take appropriate action

In general, the answer planning techniques discussed in Chapter 7 should also be applied to case study questions. So use a spider diagram or a mind map to help you to focus on the key issues and then transfer your thoughts to paper, before you write out the answer in full.

Key Point
While you must be especially conscious of the need to manage your time effectively when tackling case studies, it is worth taking a little time to refer back to the case study occasionally. Taking a look at the case study material from time to time while you are constructing your answer will refresh your memory. It will also help you to ensure that all the necessary links to the scenario are clear and fully established in your written answer.

Once your plan or diagram is complete you can begin to compose your full answer. If the question asks for the answer to be produced in 'report format' then make sure you proceed accordingly.

Guidance on how to structure your answer in 'report format' follows in Chapter 9.

Preparing coursework and assignments

Many marketing students are now required to submit coursework assignments as part of the qualification assessment process.

If you are one of these students, I'm sure you will be glad to hear that much of the guidance and advice in this book is also highly relevant and extremely applicable to assignment writing. For example, make sure you read the report writing advice in Chapter 9 before you finalise any assignments or coursework, as most (if not all) assignments should be produced in 'report format'.

Your assignment may need to be related to a given scenario as presented by your tutor, but now it's increasingly common for marketing assignments to be related to the workplace.

Key Point
When presented with an assignment brief you will usually be required to demonstrate the ability to analyse a particular marketing situation, draw conclusions and then make appropriate recommendations. Therefore the basic approach identified in Figure 8.1 should also be employed when developing and producing any type of assessed assignment or coursework.

Work-based assignments usually require you to apply the appropriate marketing theory to your own organisation or department. These practical assignments are therefore a particularly challenging test of your marketing knowledge, as well as your ability to plan, research, analyse, manage time effectively and communicate with different stakeholders in various ways. By the way, some useful time management techniques that can also be applied when planning and producing an assignment are covered in Chapter 3.

Because you will have a significant amount of time to research and develop the material for your assignment, the assessor will expect a lot from you. So you will need to take full advantage of the time and any other resources that you may be able to draw on, in order to demonstrate that you have an excellent understanding of the issues, and that you are also capable of producing a sound and focused end product in the form of a thoroughly applied practical report. If you simply produce what is often described as a 'theory dump' with little or no application, you are unlikely to gain a pass.

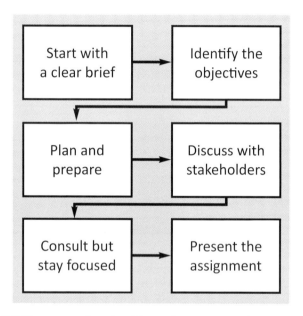

Figure 8.2 The stages involved in assignment production

The main stages involved in planning and delivering an assignment are highlighted in Figure 8.2. You must carefully read and thoroughly understand the assignment brief (ask your tutor for further advice if anything is not clear).

Having identified the associated learning objectives, competencies and performance criteria by consulting the syllabus or any assignment related documentation and noted the very important assignment submission deadline, you must then plan and prepare accordingly. This will involve managing your time, conducting the necessary research and analysing the situation, before drawing suitable conclusions and then making any appropriate recommendations.

Throughout the assignment preparation process you must take every opportunity to discuss any relevant issues with the key stakeholders (including your tutor, manager, mentor and any other appropriate individuals). When consulting anyone for advice and guidance, make sure you don't become distracted by any irrelevant ideas or suggestions some might propose, or even try to impose on you.

If you want to maximise your marks, remember that on this particular occasion the assignment assessor is the key stakeholder that you must aim to satisfy. Ideally, the end product should be a well presented and structured document prepared in a 'report format', that meets all the necessary learning aims and objectives.

> **Key Point**
> Remember that just like an exam answer, your assignment should ultimately be produced to meet the needs of the assessor. The marker will assess the content of the assignment against set marking criteria. So carefully read the brief and make sure your assignment actually meets all the necessary performance criteria.

In the case of a work-based assignment your analysis, conclusions and recommendations are likely to be of interest to your manager or employer. While various stakeholders may have an interest or even make some form of investment in your assignment if it is work-based, remember that the end product must also meet all the learning aims and objectives or performance criteria, in order for you to demonstrate the necessary skills and competencies.

If you are unduly influenced by certain stakeholders or particular work situations, your assignment might end up meeting various organisational or departmental needs, rather than those of the assessor. Of course the ideal outcome would be an assignment that demonstrates your competency, meets all the learning objectives and in addition provides your manager or employer with some useful, practical marketing-related recommendations.

At least in the case of a work-based assignment the situation is likely to be one that you are familiar with. Therefore you can take full advantage of your industry knowledge and your work-related contacts, while also utilising the knowledge, understanding and abilities identified earlier in this chapter.

> **Warning**
> All your hard work will be wasted if you don't follow the submission procedure (including completing and including any necessary paperwork with the assignment). So ensure any essential submission documentation is fully and accurately completed (you can always ask the tutor or check the Student Handbook for details if you are not sure of the procedure).

Ensure you submit the assignment correctly and on time (which in the case of international electronic submissions will mean you need to take the recipient's local time into consideration). I cannot emphasise enough how important it is for you to submit your assignment in good time, rather than leaving it until literally just before the submission deadline is due to expire.

I know quite a few students who have experienced last minute computer problems or online system failures, which prevented them from submitting their work on time.

Chapter 9 – Report writing

At one time or another, most marketing students are likely to be tested on their ability to present their findings in the form of a report.

Sometimes a particular examination question may demand that the answer is written in 'report format'. It's also common for marketing students to be asked to produce their coursework or work-based assignments in a 'report format'.

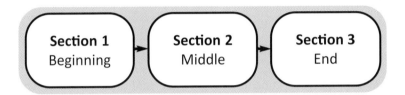

Figure 9.1 The 3 basic elements of a report

As Figure 9.1 demonstrates a report should have a clear beginning, a clear middle and a clear end. A more detailed and practical report structure that can be employed for virtually any purpose is shown in Figure 9.2.

The term 'report format' refers to the arrangement and style of a formal or informal document that is structured logically and presented clearly.

The content of such a document is typically broken down into various sections that are highlighted by appropriate headings and sub-headings (as in the case of a standard business report).

The degree of formality will depend on various factors, such as the subject or purpose of the report, the context and the industry concerned.

The following guidance on report writing is designed for readers who need to demonstrate the ability to present their findings in a report style answer in a marketing exam, an assignment, or in any typical business or work-related situation.

Formal and informal reports

Reports can vary considerably in type and style. They can be produced in either a written or oral format, which makes them available to an extremely wide readership or audience.

The remainder of this chapter focuses on the written aspect, which includes 'formal' and 'informal' reports.

It's not always easy to distinguish between formal and informal reports. Some might argue that formal reports are more methodical than informal reports, because they are produced to justify important business or commercial decisions, such as the proposed development of a new product or the planned strategic entry into new markets. There is also a view that formal reports tend to be longer than informal reports.

Some formal reports may be more comprehensive than certain informal reports and the language and terms utilised within one style of report may differ from those used in another.

Despite some of the differences that may apply all reports should be methodical, irrespective of their ultimate aim or purpose.

Every report should communicate the necessary points as clearly and as concisely as possible to the reader. After all, most readers are likely to expect an appropriate review of the key issues and few people have time to waste.

Always aim to give the readership what they want, which is likely be a clear and suitably thorough report. Every report should be logically structured and well presented, so that the contents are easy to read and absorb.

Preparation and drafting

When producing a report you can always adapt the structure and style, to match the particular circumstances and objectives involved.

The end product is more likely to meet the needs and expectations of the readers if you follow these guidelines.

Thoroughly prepare and then deliver what is required by:

• Comprehensively reading any appropriate background or supporting material (students must read the exam question or assignment brief carefully);

• Always beginning with a clear brief (students must thoroughly analyse the exam question or assignment brief, to determine exactly what is expected of them);

• Closely following the brief (students must produce a focused answer plan that can be used as the framework on which to develop the relevant sections of their report);

• Identifying and highlighting the important points (students must select the key elements from their answer plan and then emphasise and fully address the important issues in the report).

In an exam, after you have analysed the exam question, produced a suitable answer plan and identified the key points for inclusion in your report, you can then start writing your report style answer.

When preparing a report for most purposes outside the exam room, it would be important to produce a draft before completing and circulating the final version. Composing an initial draft and then checking every aspect to make sure it meets the original aims and objectives is a crucial stage of the report writing process.

Drafting and checking helps to ensure that any mistakes are corrected and all the key elements have been addressed, before the final version is produced and circulated.

Of course in the exam a draft is not appropriate or necessary, because you must produce your report style answer in full directly from your completed answer plan.

If you follow the guidelines provided in Chapter 6, you should have time to revisit your completed report style answer, if you feel the need to amend or enhance the content before the exam ends.

Structuring a report

Like any other communication a report needs to be received and understood by the recipient.

Reports should have a clear beginning (the introduction), a clear middle (the 'main body') and a clear end (the conclusions and also any associated recommendations if appropriate).

Therefore when preparing a report you should aim to:

- Follow a logical sequence;

- Address all the issues as concisely as possible;

- Incorporate clear and appropriate headings;

- Highlight any key points or other important elements;

- Incorporate figures, tables and diagrams (as appropriate);

- Include references or deadlines (if applicable).

Outside the exam room practical reports may include any number of *appendices*. A single *appendix* could take the form of one or more pages of additional information or data.

There may be numerous *appendices* involved and if so, each separate *appendix* would be allocated a number and placed in order within the *appendices* section at the end of the report.

> **Key Point**
>
> Take a look in the *Appendices* at the end of this book for a practical example of how *appendices* can be used. *Appendix 1* lists key marketing models, while *Appendix 2* lists key marketing topics.

The structure of each business report will vary according to individual preferences and the circumstances involved. However, the standard headings and sections of a typical business or management report are usually presented in the order illustrated in Figure 9.2.

Sometimes certain headings are moved around, depending on the preferences of the writer or the readers. For example, the *Executive Summary* may be located before or after the *Introduction* section.

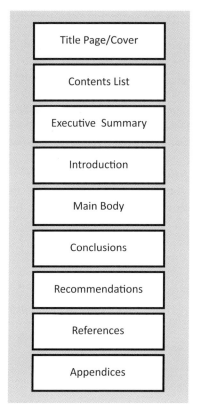

Figure 9.2 The sections of a typical report

The following example of a typical report layout does not incorporate all the elements identified in Figure 9.2, although the overall structure and format is essentially the same.

The original content of the actual report on which the following sample is based, has been replaced with some brief advice and comments. These various comments indicate what should be included in each section of a standard practical report.

A standard report *title page* or *cover sheet* as it's sometimes called is illustrated on the next page. The remaining sections of the example report follow the *title page*, as they would do in practice.

[The title of the report goes here]

Prepared for

[The name of the recipient goes here]

by

[The name of the author goes here]

[The date the report was produced goes here]

Contents

1. Introduction

2. Executive Summary

3. Results of marketing activities

4. Conclusions

5. Recommendations

6. Appendices

1. Introduction

As the above heading suggests, this first section of a report should provide a concise introduction that sets the scene for the reader.

At the beginning of some reports you are also likely to find certain relevant background information.

This opening section may contain details about the main objective(s) of the report. Sometimes the report objectives are covered under the heading *Terms of Reference*.

When a research-related report is produced the heading *Methodology* may be included towards the beginning of the report. The *Methodology* section might be incorporated within the *Introduction* section, or it may be located at the start of the 'main body'. A *Methodology* section is only required in research-based reports.

2. Executive Summary

Sometimes a brief summary of the whole report or a synopsis of the key report findings is included. If so, we call this section an *Executive Summary* and it's usually located at the beginning of a report, or immediately after the *Introduction* section. Intended to be a concise abstract, it aims to save busy readers time by providing them with a précis of the key elements of the report.

If an *Executive Summary* is incorporated within a business report, ideally it should not exceed 1 page in length. Exam answers that need to be produced in 'report format' tend not to need this particular section. One reason why an *Executive Summary* section might be included in an exam answer would be to convey that the author of the answer has an understanding of report writing techniques. If included in an exam answer, any summary would only need to be brief (otherwise valuable exam time would be wasted duplicating some of the content unnecessarily).

3. Results of marketing activities

This section is what tends to be referred to generically as the 'main body' of the report. If the report was produced in order to detail, analyse and communicate the results of recent marketing activities, this section would be given an appropriate title such as the one above.

If it was a research-based report, this section might contain details of the various questions asked and responses received. Some appropriate diagrams would no doubt be incorporated in this section, to illustrate the various results (such as pie charts, line graphs or bar charts). Some data might also be included in tabular format.

Any relevant, detailed but non-essential information that might possibly even be distracting to the reader if contained within the 'main body' of the report would be placed in the *Appendices* section.

It wouldn't be appropriate to draw conclusions or make recommendations in this 'main body' section. Many report authors seem to forget that if they are required, any conclusions and recommendations should be located in the relevant sections that follow.

This middle section is likely to be broken down into various sub-sections 'signposted' by suitable sub-headings. These individual elements of the 'main body' should be presented in a logical order, so that they clearly highlight and suitably address all the necessary points. In an exam or assignment, this section of a report style answer would be used to address many of the issues that were identified in the answer plan (answer plans can be useful when developing assignments as well as exam answers).

If required, any conclusions or recommendations should be placed in their own dedicated sections following the 'main body' of the report.

4. Conclusions

This section is where the author of the report should draw any relevant conclusions, based on the earlier analysis (if it's appropriate to do so).

Avoid the common mistake of drawing conclusions too early in the 'main body' of the report and always place them here where they belong. Some example conclusions might be as follows:

4.1 The least effective method of attracting customers was direct mail and this can be attributed to.....

4.2 The most effective method of attracting customers was local media advertising because.....

4.3 From the information obtained via the staff survey it is clear that insufficient personnel were available to deal with customer enquiries at peak times.....

You may have noticed that all the main sections of the example report are numbered. It's also possible to number sub-sections and even individual paragraphs, as illustrated by the sample conclusions provided. A highly detailed paragraph numbering approach is not necessary for general purpose reports, although when any report is being discussed it can be helpful to refer to certain sections by number.

I suggest that when preparing any report you should at least number all the main section headings, as I have done in this example.

5. Recommendations

If you are required to make some suggestions or recommendations, clearly this section is where any suitable recommendations should be proposed.

Perhaps because they are keen to communicate their ideas, some authors often start making their recommendations too early, by placing them in the 'main body' or in the *Conclusions* sections of the report, instead of locating them here in the *Recommendations* section where they belong.

There doesn't need to be exactly the same number of recommendations as there are conclusions. However, the recommendations do need to relate to the conclusions, as demonstrated by the following examples.

5.1 It is recommended that no additional direct mail activities are undertaken until the existing operation is reviewed.....

5.2 Local media advertising should continue to be used for future marketing events and further research should be conducted to determine the effects of an increased advertising spend.....

5.3 The allocation of human resources will need to be reviewed before the next event and it is recommended that planning meetings take place.....

6. Appendices

Any number of *appendices* may be included at the end of the report. An *appendix* is a document or a supplementary sheet that contains relevant information, material or resources (such as tables of data, copies of articles, advertisements, competitor-related information or any other useful details).

Any material that is considered to be optional, or that could be too distracting or time consuming to read if it were placed in the 'main body' of the report, should be located in the *appendices*. Readers then have the option to refer to the appropriate *appendices* if, and when they want.

If the author of a report needs to refer the reader to certain specific information contained in a single *appendix*, or within any number of *appendices*, this is usually done by making a suitable statement in the relevant section of the report.

For example *'these results compare favourably with the latest industry average figures contained in appendix 2'*. Readers can then go to *appendix 2* and take a look at the figures if they want.

In summary, the sections of a report should always follow a logical sequence. The content must be carefully written and structured to meet the aims and objectives identified at the start of the report, as well as the needs and expectations of the readers.

Page numbering and cover sheets

You should always number the pages of your assignment or report. Page numbering enables the reader to easily and quickly locate any specific content that must either be discussed or read.

The overall presentation and appearance of an assignment or report will benefit from the addition of a suitable *title page* or *cover sheet*.

The *cover sheet* also provides potential readers with relevant information, including the purpose of the report, who prepared it and precisely when it was prepared.

Page numbers and *cover sheets* are not essential components of a report style exam answer. However, if you have sufficient paper and time available and the exam question calls for an answer in 'report format', adding a suitable cover page at the start of the answer will convey that you understand how real reports should be presented. Any report will look more professional if it's suitably covered or bound, but never forget that the content of a report is always the most important element.

Chapter 10 – Sample exam questions

The questions in this chapter are designed to help you prepare for your final exams.

> **Key Point**
> Even though exam questions should go through a rigorous checking and refinement process before they are included in an exam paper, not every question may ultimately be 100% clear to the reader. If you must address an exam question that you feel is unclear or ambiguous, start by making a brief note to the marker that communicates the assumptions you have made and the approach you have adopted, based on your own particular interpretation of the question.

If you have any problems interpreting the *instructional* or *command* words used in the sample exam questions, refer to Chapter 12 for some further guidance on what these words actually mean.

It's essential that you have a good understanding of the meaning of the *instructional* words used by examiners. Knowing exactly what these terms mean will help you to produce more focused and precise answers, which should ultimately improve your marks.

Different levels demand different approaches

As this guide is aimed at a global readership, it must be recognised that there is likely to be some variation in the standards applied by the many marketing institutes and awarding bodies that exist worldwide. Different terms are also used to describe similar qualifications and levels of study.

The marketing certificate that you aim to gain could well be examined at the same level as the marketing diploma offered by a different institution.

Therefore I have decided to use the term 'intermediate' to refer to all middle range marketing qualifications, which includes marketing certificates and marketing diplomas.

The standalone marketing modules that often form a key part of a different industry qualification, or a profession-specific examination (such as a marketing module from a banking diploma) are also regarded as intermediate level qualifications.

Intermediate level questions

The questions in this chapter are set broadly at the intermediate level. However, if you are studying marketing at a lower or higher level don't completely ignore this section, because some of the material and guidance that follows is relevant to all levels of study.

What examiners expect at each level

Because of the variations that apply, you must do what you can to obtain the relevant information that will prescribe exactly what is required by your own examination board.

As previously mentioned in this book, make an effort to become familiar with the relevant syllabus statements and do what you can to obtain copies of past exam papers. Don't forget to take a look at any post-exam reports produced by the chief examiner or senior examiner, if they are available.

Reading the examiner's reports will give you a clear insight into the expectations, aims and requirements of your own senior examiner.

The examiner's reports will vary, but an indication of what ought to have been covered in each exam answer and a suggested approach, plus some feedback on how the answers were actually addressed in the previous exam will usually be given. Some suggestions on what could have been done to gain high marks may also be provided.

The guidance provided in the examiner's report should relate to the learning objectives and learning outcomes mentioned in the course syllabus document.

Remember that an important part of your preparation is to identify exactly what you are expected to know and what you must be able to achieve, in terms of the syllabus and the associated learning outcomes and objectives.

5 key elements that are tested in marketing exams

Figure 10.1 identifies the 5 critical components that are likely to be tested to some degree in every marketing exam.

Because certain components will be considered more important at one study level than another, the weightings for each may vary depending on the level of the exam.

1.
Presentation & communication skills

2.
Knowledge of theories & concepts

3.
Application of theories & concepts

4.
Critical analysis & justification

5.
Management planning & strategic skills

Figure 10.1 The 5 critical marketing exam components

Here's some guidance on what is likely to be tested at the various levels of study.

Studying at Level 1 – Introductory stage

At the introductory stage the emphasis is likely to be placed on testing the student's knowledge of basic marketing theory, tools and concepts. Level 1 students need to be able to convey a basic understanding of the key issues and present core concepts. Students who decide to commence their marketing studies at this level don't need any prior marketing experience or knowledge. After studying marketing at the introductory level, students should expect to have gained a basic understanding of the essentials.

Studying at Level 2 – Certificate (or equivalent) stage

As students progress to level 2 which is the lower intermediate stage, the application of theories and concepts and to a certain extent the critical analysis, evaluation and justification aspect is likely to be given more emphasis in the exam. While students don't actually need to be working in a marketing context or role when studying at this level, those who are already working in a junior or tactical position will benefit from studying at level 2.

At certificate or equivalent level, students are likely to be able to apply some of the theory and principles in their current role and later in future positions, as their career develops. After studying marketing at this level, students should expect to have gained an in-depth knowledge of a wide range of marketing issues.

Studying at Level 3 – Diploma (or equivalent) stage

At diploma level or the higher intermediate stage as it's sometimes described, students can expect to be tested much more on their ability to critically assess situations and concepts and justify views and recommendations. Students at level 3 are likely to be working in some form of marketing role and will probably already have a degree of operational responsibility. They may also have ambitions to develop their career by moving into marketing management, where they can apply the planning, implementation, measurement and control techniques they will study at level 3.

After studying marketing at the diploma level or equivalent, students should expect to have gained some knowledge of operational level planning and an appreciation of how marketing decisions can impact on stakeholders and the various business functions.

Studying at Level 4 – Postgraduate stage

The postgraduate diploma or equivalent qualification tests a student's specialist marketing knowledge at the highest level. Level 4 exam answers demand a detailed knowledge and thorough application of a wide range of relevant marketing skills and techniques. A professional approach and a sound understanding of relevant marketing management techniques is required, as well as the ability to analyse and identify the key issues and propose the most relevant strategic marketing solutions.

Those who study marketing at postgraduate level are likely to be individuals with ambitions to progress to the very top of an organisation. By succeeding at postgraduate level a marketing student will have demonstrated specialist knowledge across the subject range, plus the ability to adopt a thoroughly professional approach and a strategic perspective.

> **Key Point**
> The ability to present and communicate is an essential ingredient that plays a key role in every exam answer. While the presentation aspect may be given a different weighting at each level of study, you should always make the effort to ensure that your answers are communicated clearly and presented appropriately.

Focusing on the intermediate level requirements

Intermediate marketing students studying at levels 2 or 3 as described earlier, should expect to be tested primarily on the components in the first 4 stages identified in Figure 10.1 (to a greater or lesser degree depending on the precise level).

The components illustrated in stages 1, 2 and 3 in Figure 10.1 are likely to be given a high weighting in intermediate level exams. The 'critical analysis and justification' aspect will be tested to some degree in lower intermediate level exams and given slightly more emphasis in higher intermediate level exams.

At study levels 2 and 3 it would be risky to rely purely on outlining the relevant theory, model or concept in your answer, as such a theoretical approach alone may not be worthy of a pass.

In order to gain good marks, the knowledge and ability to demonstrate how the various concepts can actually be applied is required at intermediate level. Depending of course on what is asked in the question, a more thorough evaluation of the key issues is likely to be required as the level of study increases.

Establish exactly what is required

Remember that because of the possible variation in examination standards and requirements worldwide, ultimately it is up to you to establish exactly what your own particular institute or examination board will require.

Most institutions provide plenty of information about the skills and competencies you will need to apply and demonstrate in order to pass their exams at any given level. So always make a point of obtaining the necessary information and resources and take account of any extra advice that is made available to you.

Intermediate level questions - 3 hour exams

The sample exam style questions that follow are similar to those a marketing student might encounter in a typical 3 hour intermediate level professional marketing exam.

Aim to answer a range of these sample questions as part of your exam preparation.

Question 1

Discuss what is meant by the term Relationship Marketing and using an appropriate framework, demonstrate how the relationship with a buyer can be successfully developed by the supplier.

(20 marks)

Question 2

Summarise the original 4Ps of the marketing mix and briefly explain why it is important for marketers to understand the marketing mix concept. *(12 marks)*

Suggest why the additional 3Ps that form the extended marketing mix might have particular significance to the marketers of services.

(8 marks)

Question 3

Define the terms primary research and secondary research and detail the advantages and disadvantages of each. *(10 marks)*

Describe the various stages of the marketing research process.

(10 marks)

Question 4

Define the term market segmentation and demonstrate the benefits of a segmentation approach. *(20 marks)*

Question 5

Identify the key stakeholders of an organisation of your choice and justify their importance from a marketing perspective.

(20 marks)

Question 6

Discuss the issue of customer retention and explain why it is important. Your answer should also include suggestions on how an organisation can retain its customers. *(20 marks)*

Question 7

Illustrate and explain the various stages an individual is likely to go through when purchasing a consumer product or service.

(10 marks)

Describe the consumer DMU and briefly explain why an understanding of this concept is important to marketers. *(10 marks)*

Question 8

Discuss the view that the modern consumer is very different from the customers of the past. *(20 marks)*

Question 9

Demonstrate the differences between marketing a physical product and marketing a typical service. *(20 marks)*

Question 10

Assess the value of analysing the competition. *(8 marks)*

Illustrate an appropriate framework that could be used to analyse the competitive forces that exist within the external micro environment. *(12 marks)*

Question 11

Examine the use and benefits of technology-based marketing.

(20 marks)

Question 12

Define the 4Cs of the marketing mix and compare and contrast the 4Cs model with an alternative version of the marketing mix.

(20 marks)

Question 13

Detail the promotional mix and using examples, explain how the various elements of the promotional mix can be used effectively.

(20 marks)

Question 14

Using relevant examples distinguish between the following types of purchase decision and explain why marketers should make an effort to understand buyer behaviour:

- Impulse;

- Routine;

- Emotional;

- Rational. *(20 marks)*

Question 15

Describe the Ansoff matrix and using examples demonstrate how it can be used by marketers. *(20 marks)*

Question 16

Illustrate the Product Life Cycle and demonstrate its value to marketers. *(20 marks)*

Question 17

Examine the term total product concept and discuss its relevance to marketers. *(10 marks)*

Define branding and discuss its value to marketers. *(10 marks)*

Question 18

Discuss the view that price is the most important element of the marketing mix. *(10 marks)*

Assess the value of physical evidence from a marketing perspective. *(10 marks)*

Question 19

Using examples identify and discuss 3 different brand strategies. *(12 marks)*

Explain the following terms:

- Brand extension;

- Brand stretching;

- Re-branding. *(8 marks)*

Question 20

Using relevant examples, distinguish between consumer buyer behaviour and organisational buyer behaviour. *(20 marks)*

Question 21

Describe the new product development process.   *(12 marks)*

Suggest how an organisation might go about obtaining new ideas.
(8 marks)

Question 22

Illustrate and review Maslow's hierarchy of needs concept.
(20 marks)

Question 23

Suggest how a firm selling to consumers (B2C) might segment the market.   *(10 marks)*

Define the term positioning and assess its value to marketers.
(10 marks)

Question 24

Summarise the distribution channel options that are available to a firm of your choice.   *(10 marks)*

Identify the factors that should be considered by an organisation when selecting a new distribution channel.   *(10 marks)*

Question 25

Illustrate and explain the stages of the organisational buying process.   *(10 marks)*

Describe a typical organisational DMU and briefly explain how it differs from the consumer model.   *(10 marks)*

Question 26

Discuss the common positioning strategies and describe the common positioning errors. Use examples to illustrate your points.
(20 marks)

Question 27

Outline a suitable framework that marketers can use as the basis for creating a marketing plan. *(12 marks)*

Explain why it is important to plan. *(8 marks)*

Question 28

Explain the purpose of marketing objectives. *(8 marks)*

Suggest the typical marketing objectives that are likely to be set by a large mass market organisation, such as a supermarket or a well-known high street retailer. *(12 marks)*

Question 29

Explain the process of product and service adoption. *(10 marks)*

Summarise the characteristics of customers at each stage of the adoption process. *(10 marks)*

Question 30

Identify and discuss an appropriate framework that could be used by marketers to analyse the external macro environment.
(10 marks)

Explain the significance of pressure groups as stakeholders and how these might affect a marketing organisation. *(10 marks)*

These sample questions cover a range of popular and important marketing issues. So take full advantage of this unique and valuable opportunity to develop your question analysis, answer planning and writing skills.

Additional sample exam questions online

For an update, including details of alternative sample exam style questions that can also be answered and submitted for marking visit *www.garydavies.com/questions.*

Gain some practice before the exam

Even if you don't submit any of the questions in this book for marking and feedback, you should still aim to address as many sample questions as you can. Try to gain as much question answering experience as your busy schedule will allow before you sit your exam.

> **Key Point**
> Investing some of your valuable time in answering typical questions before the exam will benefit you in many ways. So don't forget to build sufficient hours into your study plan for this important and worthwhile task.

Answering exam style questions within realistic timeframes will probably expose a few gaps in your subject knowledge. Any weaknesses that are highlighted can usually be eliminated quickly and easily, by undertaking some appropriate reading and research.

Practice putting pen to paper

Most professional exams still require students to produce answers in a handwritten format and this can be a real challenge for some. Many of us now rely on information technology and therefore we type emails, letters and reports when we need to communicate in writing, rather than using a pen and paper. This means that when we find ourselves under pressure to produce detailed handwritten answers quickly in the exam, our rarely used handwriting skills can occasionally let us down.

When you need to write something like a short personal letter, your handwriting is no doubt reasonably neat and legible. However, from experience I know that during a 3 hour exam most people's handwriting is likely to deteriorate at some point, even though it may be fairly neat and tidy at the beginning of the script.

Key Point
Try answering 5 sample questions in 3 hours (this is a typical professional marketing exam format) and then take a look at your handwriting once you have answered all the questions.

To test your handwriting under exam conditions answer a few questions allowing yourself 30 minutes to complete each answer, just like you would in the exam. Then take an objective look at the end result to see if your handwriting is clearly legible throughout.

If you are honest with yourself, you may decide that parts of your answer might need to be read more than once in order for the reader to be able to identify the key points. If that is the case, aim to improve your handwriting.

Most students naturally focus on gaining an appropriate knowledge and understanding of the subject, but few consider what their exam answers will look like when viewed from the marker's perspective. Clear and neat handwriting certainly creates a good impression, but more importantly it assists the marker.

Chapter 11 – Submission procedure

You can submit any of the questions in Chapter 10 for marking and feedback.

> **Key Point**
> If you want to take advantage of the marking and feedback option, all you need to do is read the following guidelines carefully and follow the instructions provided.

Updates including details of any alternative exam style questions can be found online at *www.garydavies.com/questions*.

Replicating exam conditions

Before taking a look at the submission procedure in detail, let's give some thought to the approaches that you might adopt when answering these sample exam style questions.

It may be best for you to replicate exam conditions and set a realistic timeframe, by allocating an appropriate amount of time to answer each sample question (as you would in the exam). If so, you could allocate yourself approximately 30 minutes to answer each question, depending on the type of exam you plan to sit.

Adopting a strict timed approach when answering sample questions may well put you under some pressure and the quality of your answers might suffer. However, by working within a typical exam-related timeframe, you will certainly find out what it's like to have to produce sound answers quickly.

Alternatively, you might feel it's best for you to undertake some additional specific reading and research and then work on your answer over a much longer period of time.

Allowing yourself more time to answer the question may engender a false sense of security and won't actually prepare you for working under pressure in the actual exam. However, allowing plenty of time to read around a topic and conduct further research will no doubt broaden your knowledge and improve your understanding of the subject.

Each approach has its pros and cons. So if you answer a number of sample exam questions, perhaps you can vary the approach depending on what you want to gain from the process.

The main aim should be to gain plenty of practice answering exam style questions before you sit the exam!

Question submission procedure

If you would like your answers to the sample questions in this book marked by a qualified and experienced marketing examiner, all you need to do is follow the submission procedure outlined in Figure 11.1.

Once your answers are received and provided you have followed the guidelines correctly, they will be marked and returned to you with some suitable constructive feedback, designed to help you maximise your marks in the final exam.

Please follow the answer submission guidelines carefully. I suggest you approach this process in the same way that you plan to follow the instructions in your actual exam.

Your sample exam answers may not be marked and returned, or delays may occur if you do not follow the submission procedure.

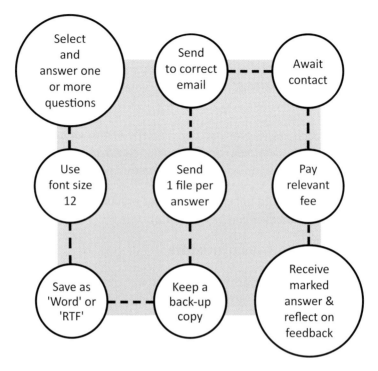

Figure 11.1 The answer submission process

Electronic submission is recommended because it's cheaper and quicker than the other submission methods. Therefore if possible you should aim to follow the electronic submission process enumerated on the following pages.

1) Fully answer the question or questions of your choice, after applying the question analysis and answer planning techniques covered in this guide.

2) Type your answers using a suitable word processing software package. Make sure the page size is set to A4, use single spacing, preferably a font size of 12 and ideally either a 'Calibri', 'Times

New Roman' or 'Arial' font for the man body text.

3) Save your exam answers in either a Microsoft 'Word' format, or in the 'RTF' format to ensure your answer document can be opened and viewed correctly (most word processing software packages allow you to save a document in 'RTF' format).

4) Remember to save at least 1 copy of your electronic answer as a back-up in case of any unforeseen or unexpected problems (*please note responsibility will not be accepted for any loss of data, information or other assets or resources as a result of any problems associated with the transmission of electronic documents or files, so ensure you always keep a back-up copy of any files you submit*).

5) Use a separate document file for each individual exam answer that you submit. For example, if you submit 1 answer email a single file attachment containing your answer. If you submit 3 different answers at the same time, then send just 1 email that incorporates 3 separate file attachments.

6) Send your email and the associated file attachment or attachments in the correct file format (either 'Word' or 'RTF) to *submissions@garydavies.com*.

7) Wait for a personal email response to confirm your submission has been received for marking and feedback. The confirmation email will provide you with a link to an online payment system.

8) Once you receive the confirmation email you should follow the instructions provided in the message, then visit the specified online payment system and pay the appropriate marking fee. This will ensure that your assignment is marked and returned without any delay. You will be provided with details of alternative payment methods in the email. Information on current marking fees and any other associated matters can be obtained by emailing

info@garydavies.com or by visiting the dedicated website at *www.garydavies.com/marking.*

9) Your marked exam answer or answers will be returned together with some appropriate feedback within the stated timeframe. For more information and an update on the turnaround times visit *www.garydavies.com/marking.*

10) If you need your exam answers marked and returned more quickly than normal, email *info@garydavies.com* to request details of the fast-track marking and feedback facility.

11) If you experience any problems while following the above procedure, or if you have any other questions or concerns, visit *www.garydavies.com/marking* or email *info@garydavies.com* for assistance.

Don't forget to follow all the advice provided earlier on how to present and structure your exam answers. You might want to take another look at the relevant sections of Chapters 6 and 7 to refresh your memory, before you attempt to answer any questions.

Note that the typical turnaround time for marked answers could occasionally be affected by various factors such as public holidays. For an update on any issues that may affect the standard turnaround times you can visit *www.garydavies.com/marking* or email *info@garydavies.com* in advance of any planned submission to check the current situation.

When you receive any marked answer or assignment

When your marked answer is returned, always read the feedback comments carefully. Take a little time to think objectively about the issues that have been raised by the marker. Then reflect positively on the constructive feedback and any advice that has been provided. Make sure you act on the advice you receive, in order to improve your knowledge and your overall answering approach.

If the marks you gained were at the lower end of the scale, think positively and congratulate yourself for making the sensible decision to submit the answer for marking and feedback.

At least by obtaining a mark and some feedback you will have gained the chance to put things right before the exam (which is an important part of your pre-exam preparation).

If your answer was rewarded with relatively high marks, give yourself a well deserved pat on the back. High marks are not easy to achieve and they usually come as a result of hard work over time, so well done.

However, be careful that you don't let any initial success go to your head and never fall into the trap of becoming too confident. Over confidence, complacency and taking future results for granted is dangerous and therefore should be avoided. Sustain the effort and keep up the good work, so that you can maintain an air of cautious optimism when you enter the exam room on the day.

If your marks were more or less average, then at least you have established a good foundation on which you can build.

However, don't assume that because you may have gained what might equate to a pass mark in your pre-exam preparation that you don't need to do any more work. If you find you have achieved an average grade for any of the sample answers you have submitted for marking before the exam, it's best to work on the basis that a degree of improvement is still necessary (just to be on the safe side).

If you prefer not to submit the sample questions for marking, of course you can still work through them. At least by doing this you will gain some valuable practice in analysing, planning and answering exam style questions.

Chapter 12 – Instructional words

Always pay careful attention to the instructions you receive from the senior examiner.

Key Point
Senior examiners are likely to use certain carefully selected words in the exam questions they generate. Each of these words demands that you should follow a particular direction, or a certain course of action. That's why they are referred to as *instructional* or *command* words.

Some examples of the *instructional* or *command* words used by examiners in exam questions are identified in Figure 12.1.

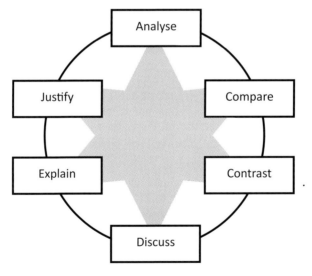

Figure 12.1 Examples of instructional or command words

To maximise your marks you must make sure that you follow these specific commands and give the markers exactly what they need.

While you can never be certain that a senior examiner will construct questions that follow any set *instructional* word guidelines, most exam questions are likely to incorporate popular *instructional* words, such as those outlined in the remainder of this chapter.

Common instructional words used by senior examiners

Word	Meaning
Advise	Offer your own recommendations.
Amplify	Expand upon or develop a particular statement, quotation or other issue.
Analyse	Thoroughly examine the components of a theory, concept, environment or other issue.
Appraise	Assess the importance, significance or value, based on the perceived strengths and weaknesses.
Argue	Highlight the reasons for or against a topic, or a particular course of action based on evidence.
Assess	Estimate the importance, significance or value of an issue, concept or situation using a suitable framework.
Clarify	Clearly present or communicate complicated, vague or unexplored issues.
Comment	Remark on the issue or situation based on the factual evidence, data or information provided.
Compare	Identify both the similarities and the differences that apply to two or more distinct elements, issues or approaches.

Consider	Carefully think about and then communicate the particular merits of an issue or situation.
Contrast	Identify and highlight the opposing differences.
Criticise	Analyse and then communicate the faults in a given theory, view or opinion.
Define	Provide a precise explanation of the exact meaning.
Demonstrate	Offer logical proof using an appropriate example.
Describe	Present a detailed account incorporating the significant points and characteristics.
Detail	Meticulously specify the key points or issues.
Discuss	Examine a topic from various different perspectives, comment on the pros and cons through the use of logical argument (similar to 'compare and contrast').
Distinguish	Highlight the key differences between one issue, element or approach and another.
Enumerate	Create a numbered list of the relevant items.
Evaluate	Assess the strengths and weaknesses of a theory, or give your opinion following an appraisal based on selected criteria.
Examine	Thoroughly investigate the particular theory, statement or other issue.
Explain	Clearly specify the meaning using logic.
Explore	Investigate and examine in order to find out more.

Identify	Analyse and then present the stated issue.
Illustrate	Clarify an issue by providing specific examples or comparisons (usually by drawing a chart, diagram or graph).
Interpret	Evaluate the relevant issue, approach or statement and then clearly communicate the meaning or significance in your own words.
Justify	Present sufficient grounds for a specific action, strategy, tactic, view or approach (often by referring to other sources or evidence).
List	Put together in order by placing each subsequent entry below the other (as in the case of a 'bullet point' list or a numerical list).
Outline	Provide an overview of the main issues, facts or ideas.
Propose	Suggest an idea, point of view, approach, argument or course of action.
Prove	Verify the accuracy of a given action, strategy, tactic, view or approach based on fact.
Reconcile	Demonstrate how two apparently conflicting statements or theories can actually be similar or compatible.
Relate	Highlight the various connections or associations between separate points, ideas or events.
Review	Undertake an assessment or appraisal involving critical analysis and personal judgement.

Show	Demonstrate the reality of the situation utilising available evidence.
State	Communicate the issue clearly, or provide a precise explanation.
Suggest	Propose the most appropriate recommendations, or present the most suitable ideas.
Summarise	Provide a concise, refined account of the key points.
Trace	Track the development of a theory, or illustrate the order of events.

More about the author

This section has been included for readers who would like to know a little more about the author. Gary has worked successfully for many years in sales, marketing, management, education and training. He took his first important career step when he became a young sales representative in the financial services and banking sector back in 1973.

After gaining various promotions, changing roles and working in different industrial sectors (including spending many enjoyable and rewarding years as a lecturer in marketing, management and business) Gary became the general manager of a Science Park.

He left the Science Park to establish his own training, consultancy and writing business. Since then he has developed an international client list and worked with numerous sales, marketing, management and business students and delegates, teaching, training and providing examination advice and support.

Gary has worked as an examiner, a senior examiner and a chief examiner on a range of sales and marketing qualifications for various internationally known and respected professional institutions. He has written the questions for the exams, managed the marking teams, marked and sampled the exam scripts and prepared the post-examination reports.

In addition to holding relevant professional qualifications Gary has considerable experience in sales, marketing, business, management and leadership. His practical experience was gained throughout a long, diverse and successful career, although his professional qualifications were all obtained relatively late in life.

The qualifications Gary gained as a full-time and part-time mature student include the following:

- Masters Degree in Business Administration (MBA);
- Chartered Institute of Marketing Certificate;
- Chartered Institute of Marketing Advanced Certificate;
- Chartered Institute of Marketing Diploma (DipM);
- Institute of Export Professional Qualifications.

Following his mid-career decision to resign from a secure job in order to undertake a concentrated period of full-time study, Gary was subsequently awarded 'Mature Student of the Year'.

During his first year as a mature student he was also presented with a certificate of 'Exceptional Proficiency' by the Lord Mayor of London, for his performance in the professional examinations.

These early modest academic successes as a mature student, after what can best be described as an undistinguished performance at grammar school many years earlier, encouraged Gary to pursue his professional studies further and ultimately changed the direction of his career.

More about Gary, including his latest projects and forthcoming books can be found at *www.garydavies.com*.

Appendix 1 – A to Z list of key marketing models

Here is a list of the key marketing models, concepts, tools and frameworks that you should aim to be familiar with at the intermediate level of study:

4Cs - version of the 'marketing mix' that places the emphasis on the customer perspective;

4Ps - original version of the 'marketing mix';

5Ms - model that highlights the stages involved in planning and developing an advertising or promotional campaign;

7Ps - extended version of the 'marketing mix' aka 'extended marketing mix' or the 'service marketing mix';

AIDA – basic communications design tool;

Ansoff matrix - model that highlights 4 basic marketing strategies developed by Dr.H.I.Ansoff;

Boston matrix - tool used to analyse the product portfolio (designed for analysing strategic business units) aka 'BCG' matrix;

Diffusion of innovation - model that illustrates the adoption of a product or service by different customer types over time;

Loyalty ladder - framework associated with customer relationship development and customer loyalty;

Marketing audit - framework used to assess the marketing elements and systems within a given organisation;

Marketing mix - marketing model that highlights the essential components of marketing (there are different versions including the '4Ps', the '7Ps' and the '4Cs');

Maslow's hierarchy of needs - concept that highlights a range of human needs identified by Professor A.H.Maslow;

New product development process – key stages involved in developing a new product or service and bringing it to the market;

PESTLE - tool used to analyse the macro environment (the political, economic, social, technological, legal and eco-environmental influences within the far external environment);

Porter's 5 forces - framework that highlights the influences which determine industry profitability, developed by Professor M.E.Porter;

Porter's generic strategies - model that identifies core strategies, which each offer a different route to competitive advantage, developed by Professor M.E.Porter;

Product life cycle - concept that highlights the various stages a typical product is said to follow from conception to withdrawal;

Promotional mix - term used to describe the various communications that make up the 'promotion' element of the marketing mix, aka 'communications mix';

Service marketing mix - extended version of the 'marketing mix', aka 'extended marketing mix' or the '7Ps';

Total product concept - model that highlights the different elements and potential complexity of a given product or service.

Appendix 2 – A to Z list of key marketing topics

Here is a list of key marketing topics, terms and subject areas that you should aim to be familiar with at the intermediate level of study:

Advertising and advertising agencies;

Branding and brand strategies;

Budgeting;

Buyer behaviour;

Communications mix (aka 'promotional mix');

Competitive strategies and competitor analysis;

Corporate social responsibility;

Customer relationship management;

Decision making process;

Decision making unit;

Desk research (aka 'secondary research');

Direct marketing;

Distribution channels;

Ethical, societal and 'green' marketing;

Extended marketing mix (aka 'service marketing mix');

Field research (aka 'primary research');

Growth and use of technologies;

Internal environment and analysis;

Internal marketing;

International marketing;

Macro environment (far external environment) and analysis;

Market intelligence;

Market orientation;

Market research (component of 'marketing research');

Market segmentation (aka 'segmentation');

Marketing audit;

Marketing channels;

Marketing communications;

Marketing concept;

Marketing mix;

Marketing orientation;

Marketing research agencies;

Marketing research methods;

Marketing research process;

Marketing strategies and tactics;

Micro environment (near external environment) and analysis;

New product development process;

Positioning;

Price and pricing strategies;

Product portfolio analysis;

Project management;

Promotional mix (aka 'communications mix');

Relationship marketing;

Segmentation (aka 'market segmentation');

Service marketing (non-product marketing);

Service marketing mix (expanded version of the 'marketing mix', aka 'extended marketing mix' or the '7Ps');

Stakeholder analysis;

Stakeholder marketing;

Targeting;

Transactional marketing;

Viral marketing.